DALE SCARBO...

THE VIETNAM WAR IN CONTEXT

HODDER
EDUCATION
AN HACHETTE UK COMPANY

Dedication
For Jacob R. Helmes

Acknowledgements
The author and publisher would like to thank Dr David Milne, University of East Anglia, for his enthusiasm and friendliness in acting as academic consultant. All judgements, interpretations and errors remain the responsibility of the author. The author would also like to thank Ian Dawson for his encouragement and patience.

Photo credits
Cover © Gary Blakeley/Fotolia

p.4 © Dale Scarboro; p.5 © LBJ Library photo by Yoichi R. Okamoto; p.6 © Larry Burrows/Time Magazine/The LIFE Picture Collection/ Getty Images; p.9 top © US Air Force/Getty Images, left © Library of Congress, Prints & Photographs Division, LC-USZ62-117124, centre © Bettmann/Corbis, right © Jerry Tavin/Everett/REX; p.10 left © ArenaCreative/Fotolia, right © Vacclav/Fotolia; p.11 left © bbourdages/Fotolia, top right © Tim Page/Corbis, bottom right © Corbis; p.16 © Georgios Kollidas/Fotolia; p.17 top © Oscar White/Corbis, centre © Library of Congress, Prints & Photographs Division, LC-USZ62-117124, bottom © Bettmann/Corbis; p. 18 © Archive Photos/Getty Images; p.22 © Keystone/Getty Images; p.27 © Henri Huet/AP/Press Association Images; p.29 © AP/Press Association Images; p.30 © US Mint; p.31 © Solo Syndication/ Associated Newspapers Ltd./ Cartoon by Vicky (Victor Weisz), Evening Standard January 8, 1964, British Cartoon Archive, University of Kent, www.cartoons.ac.uk; p.34 © US Army Photo/ Alamy; pp. 39, 55, left 99, 126, © Dale Scarboro; p.42 © Bettmann/ Corbis; p.47 © Dale Scarboro; p.48 © Punch Limited; p.54 © AP/ Press Association Images; p.56 top © Universal History Archive/ Getty Images, bottom © John Filo/AP/Press Association Images; p.57 top © Larry Burrows/The LIFE Images Collection/Getty Images, bottom © Ronald S. Haeberle/The LIFE Picture Collection/Getty Images; p.58 top © Eddie Adams/AP/Press Association Images, bottom © Nick Ut/AP/Press Association Images; p.67 © Everett Collection Historical/Alamy; p.77 © Bettmann/Corbis; p.84 © Rolls Press/Popperfoto/Getty Images; p.86 'I Want Out', anti-Vietnam War poster (colour litho), American School, (20th century)/Private Collection/© Peter Newark American Pictures/Bridgeman Images; p.89 © Rolls Press/Popperfoto/Getty Images; p.91 left © Jerry Tavin/ Everett/REX, centre © Mondadori Portfolio/Getty Images, right © Rue des Archives/AGIP/Getty Images; p.99 top © Courtesy Everett Collection/REX, bottom right © Universal/Everett/REX; p.100 top © Courtesy Everett Collection/REX, centre © Courtesy Everett Collection/REX, bottom © Everett/REX Shutterstock; p.102 © Roger Viollet/Getty Images; p.105 left © Ullstein Bild via Getty Images, right © Fotosearch/Getty Images; p.111 all © Dale Scarboro; p.117 © HO/Reuters/Corbis; p.118 left © Hulton Archive/Getty Images, right © The US National Archives and Records Administration; p.119 © Sovfoto/UIG via Getty Images; p.120 left © CSU Archives/ Everett Collection/REX, right © Oscar White/Corbis; p.127 © JIJI PRESS/AFP/Getty Images; p.133 left & right © Dale Scarboro

Every effort has been made to trace all copyright holders, but if any have been inadvertently overlooked, the Publishers will be pleased to make the necessary arrangements at the first opportunity.

The Schools History Project
Set up in 1972 to bring new life to history for students aged 13–16, the Schools History Project continues to play an innovatory role in secondary history education. From the start, the SHP aimed to show how good history has an important contribution to make to the education of a young person. It does this by creating courses and materials which both respect the importance of up-to-date, well-researched history and provide enjoyable learning experiences for students.

Since 1978 the Project has been based at Trinity and All Saints University College Leeds. It continues to support, inspire and challenge teachers through the annual conference, regional courses and website: http://www.schoolshistoryproject.org.uk. The Project is also closely involved with government bodies and awarding bodies in the planning of courses for Key Stage 3, GCSE and A level.

For teacher support material for this title, visit www.schoolshistoryproject.org.uk.

Although every effort has been made to ensure that website addresses are correct at time of going to press, Hodder Education cannot be held responsible for the content of any website mentioned in this book. It is sometimes possible to find a relocated web page by typing in the address of the home page for a website in the URL window of your browser.

Hachette UK's policy is to use papers that are natural, renewable and recyclable products and made from wood grown in sustainable forests. The logging and manufacturing processes are expected to conform to the environmental regulations of the country of origin.

Orders: please contact Bookpoint Ltd, 130 Milton Park, Abingdon, Oxon OX14 4SB. Telephone: +44 (0)1235 827720. Fax: +44 (0)1235 400454. Lines are open 9.00a.m.–5.00p.m., Monday to Saturday, with a 24-hour message answering service. Visit our website at www.hoddereducation.co.uk.

© Dale Scarboro 2015
First published in 2015 by
Hodder Education,
an Hachette UK company
338 Euston Road
London NW1 3BH

Impression number	10	9	8	7	6	5	4	3	2	1
Year			2019	2018	2017	2016	2015			

Typeset in 10pt Usherwood Book by DC Graphic Design Ltd., Hextable, Kent
Artwork by DC Graphic Design Ltd.
Printed and bound in Italy.

A catalogue record for this title is available from the British Library

ISBN 978 1 4718 0864 7

Contents

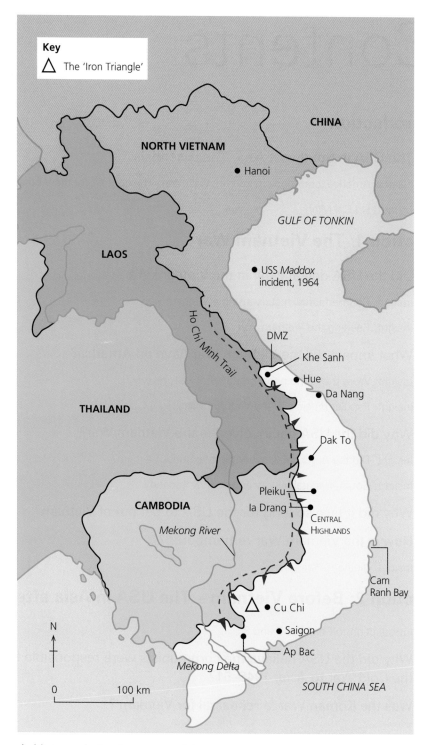

△ Vietnam during the course of the war.

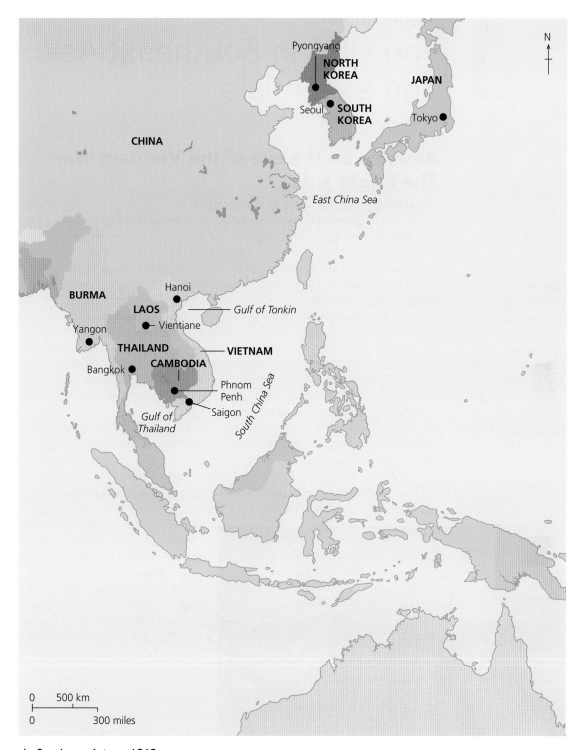

△ Southeast Asia, c. 1965.

1 The USA in Southeast Asia: The essentials

America on the eve of the Vietnam War: The bright side

1964 was a good year to be an American.

Middle class
Neither rich nor poor.

For the large **middle class**, the standard of living was higher than ever before. West Germany and Japan did not yet challenge America's dominance of the world market. American industry supported a boom in consumerism fuelled by ingenious TV advertisements, low property prices and cheap petrol. In 1964 the first Ford Mustang, the original **muscle car**, rolled off the assembly line.

Muscle car
An American high-performance, two-door sport coupe with rear-wheel drive and four seats, like the 1969 Dodge Charger. The high-speed car chase in the film *Bullitt* features two muscle cars.

America was still a small-town society. Children played outdoors without a thought for their safety, went out on Halloween without adult supervision and watched Saturday morning TV cartoons. At the movies they watched family entertainments such as *My Fair Lady*, *Godzilla* movies, and *It's A Mad, Mad, Mad, Mad World* (my personal favourite). In 1964 the Beatles came to America and appeared on the *Ed Sullivan Show*, a landmark in American popular culture.

On a national level, too, America was making progress. In 1964 Dr Martin Luther King received the Nobel Peace Prize, Sidney Poitier became the first black man to win an Oscar for Best Actor, and Congress passed the 1964 Civil Rights Act. Lyndon Johnson launched his ambitious Great Society programme to end poverty in America, and won the presidential election with a landslide victory. Even the Cold War seemed to be going

well. America was finally taking the lead from the Russians in the space race. In 1962 America faced down the Soviet Union in the Cuban Missile Crisis, and now relations with the Russians seemed to be improving: an international treaty banned the atmospheric testing of nuclear weapons.

In November 1964 my family was chosen as Family of the Year by our local newspaper, the *Bristol Virginia-Tennessean*, as part of the pre-Christmas advertising drive. Photographers from the paper followed us around town and pictured us in a series of fictitious scenarios, purchasing a stereo hi-fi and diamond jewellery, and drinking Coca-Cola and egg-nog. They came into our home and photographed us reading the paper – that's me on the floor, second from the left, reading the funny papers. For me this picture captures the essence of America in 1964 – the relaxed prosperity, the strong family unit, Christmas consumerism.

America on the eve of the Vietnam War: The dark side

Three months before this picture was taken, an American destroyer was attacked by North Vietnamese torpedo boats in the Gulf of Tonkin, the first act in the drama that led America directly into the Vietnam War. Not that we would have known much about it from the *Bristol Virginia-Tennessean*: in 1964 there was not a single American newspaper published coast to coast. Local papers like ours focused on local news – weddings, car crashes, high-school football games. International news was usually buried inside the paper, out of sight, out of mind.

The man in the centre of this photograph is Lyndon Johnson, president of the United States from 22 November 1963 until 20 January 1969. Johnson came to the presidency in tragic circumstances. On 22 November 1963 he was travelling in the car immediately behind President Kennedy's when Kennedy was assassinated. As the shots rang out, a secret service agent threw himself over Johnson as his car sped off to Parkland Hospital behind Kennedy's limousine. Johnson and his wife were ushered into a windowless room inside the hospital with armed secret service men in attendance. Minutes passed like hours. Then someone came into the room. His first words were, 'Mr President…'. Johnson knew then that Kennedy was dead.

△ Lyndon Johnson, Dean Rusk and Robert McNamara.

All his life Johnson had wanted to be president of the USA – but not like this. The assassination placed Johnson in a terrible quandary. Whenever he made a decision, people asked themselves: 'What would Kennedy have done?' None of these decisions was more important, or more difficult, than the problem facing him in Vietnam. By 1963 there were 16,000 American advisors in Vietnam. In 1961 Kennedy had promised that America would support countries like South Vietnam against the spread of communism. Now that country faced invasion from the communist North, and a communist uprising in the South. Should America send its own troops to defend South Vietnam?

Hubris and truth

This photograph was taken in 1965 when the US Marines stormed onto the coast of South Vietnam. It looks like photos taken during the Second World War when the Marines landed on Japanese-held islands in the Pacific. During the Second World War these landings were difficult and costly: at Iwo Jima over 7,800 Americans were killed taking the island. No-one was injured when the Marines landed at Da Nang in 1965.

The landing was staged for dramatic effect. Most of the Marines landed from transport ships or in cargo planes, but an amphibious landing carried the message that the United States Marine Corps had arrived. Surely the enemy would simply melt away when they faced the **Green Machine**. Anyway, the soldiers did not face opposition when they hit the beach. Beautiful South Vietnamese girls met them and placed flowers around their necks. It was as if they had already won.

Green Machine
The United States Marine Corps.

The war that followed – the Vietnam War – was one of the ugliest, longest, least successful wars in American history. It was, perhaps, the loneliest war American soldiers have ever fought. It had a way of forcing people to make difficult decisions, as the following story illustrates.

Decisions, decisions

John Ketwig was an ordinary soldier – a private – in the US Army. Someone told him that if you enlisted you were sent to Germany, but if you were drafted you were sent to Vietnam. Ketwig enlisted and got sent to Vietnam anyway.

In November 1967 he was serving as a mechanic. A major battle was being fought at Dak To, the airstrip was out of action and the 4th Division needed ammunition. One morning the sergeant came in and asked for volunteers to drive ammo to Dak To. Ketwig volunteered. Since arriving in Vietnam he had feared battle. Afraid that he would let everyone down when it came, he decided to get it over with in the company of strangers.

He was driving a big 1.5 ton truck. Sitting on his right was an experienced soldier he called Shotgun, riding shotgun to protect the convoy. They set off up the road in pouring rain, the truck grinding up through the gears and the mud, following a flat-bed truck loaded with ammunition. Suddenly there was a huge explosion. Ketwig described what happened next:

There was a giant confusion up ahead, a curtain of mud, a blinding flash, a roar unlike anything I had ever heard. I couldn't see. I couldn't hear. I existed in a slow-motion world turned upside down … The wiper cut through the wash of mud, and I glimpsed a dark hole and went for it. We plunged in, and we came out, and I was out of control, and there was a giant dark green truck stopped dead in the road. Nothing to do, nowhere to go, a dead-end tunnel; then limbs and leaves pounding against the windshield, popping, scraping, tearing; and I can't see; and … we were stopped. I sat, deflated and baffled. Frozen. I became aware of a frantic activity and confusion. I became aware that I was alive. Like a surreal movie, a face appeared to my right; a distorted, anguished face, obviously screaming, but I couldn't hear what it was saying. Where was Shotgun…? Where had he gone?

There was a guy, lying in the mud, with a stick … and an abstract swarm of golden insects flew away from his head, and I concentrated on the crackling sound because it must be a clue; the stick was his rifle, and he was shooting, and the insects were shell casings, and the roar was a lot of explosive, and we were hit…

Suddenly Shotgun was there, screaming, hugging me, slapping my back, raving at the top of his lungs. '… mother****** had our name on it, and you f***** drove that f***** truck and we f***** made it, and … and … f*****-A! F***** Christ, man, you f***** did it, you f*****-A did it, man…'

The flatbed just ahead of us had hit a mine. The whole load of ammo went off. Somebody said we went through it on two wheels, just from the force of the concussion. Blew that big f***** hole in the road. Dented the jungle. The guys in the truck? They were looking for them, for something to send home.

On that day in November 1967 Ketwig made a decision that nearly cost him his life. He survived the war and wrote a book about it. He called his book …*and a hard rain fell*, a reference to Bob Dylan's prophetic song, **Hard Rain**.

No-one can really understand modern America without knowing about Vietnam. And yet, the Vietnam War is passing into history. Today it is hard to see how Vietnam could ever have been a threat to America's national security.

Hard Rain
One of Dylan's most famous protest songs. It warns that we are on the brink of disaster.

The American war in Vietnam: An outline

For America, the Vietnam War fell into three distinct phases:

Phase 1: advisers, 1961–63. President Kennedy sent US military advisers to help the South Vietnamese officers fight the war. By the time Kennedy died in November 1963 the USA had 16,000 military advisers in South Vietnam.

Phase 2: escalation, 1964–68. President Johnson sent more and more US troops to Vietnam. By the time he left office in January 1969 there were nearly 550,000 US soldiers in Vietnam. US forces were commanded by General Westmoreland until 1968. His basic strategy was attrition – to engage enemy forces in large battles that permitted American firepower to kill so many communists that they would give up. He calculated that Americans could kill communists in the ratio of 1:12.

Phase 3: 'Vietnamisation', 1969–73. President Nixon gradually handed the war back over to the South Vietnamese Army. This phase ended with the removal of all US combat troops in 1973, followed by the final defeat of South Vietnam in 1975. US forces were commanded by General Abrams from 1968 until 1972. He abandoned Westmoreland's strategy of attrition in favour of what he called the 'One War' strategy involving greater cooperation between the American and South Vietnamese armies. He also placed greater emphasis on training the South Vietnamese Army to take over when the Americans left.

This timeline opposite is to help you understand these phases. It also shows you the rise and fall of US casualties in Vietnam and major battles referred to in the rest of this book.

Containing communism in the Cold War

The purpose of the Vietnam War was to stop the spread of communism in Southeast Asia. This was part of the much larger global strategy of **containment** begun in 1947 at the beginning of the Cold War. This started in Europe after the Second World War when the Soviet Union forced Eastern European countries to have communist governments. In 1949 China also became a communist country, which threatened to spread communism to Asian countries. Between 1950 and 1953 America fought the Korean War to defend South Korea from an invasion by the communist North. The Vietnam War was another war fought in Asia to stop the spread of communism. As shown on pages 10–11, America paid a high price for its wars in Asia.

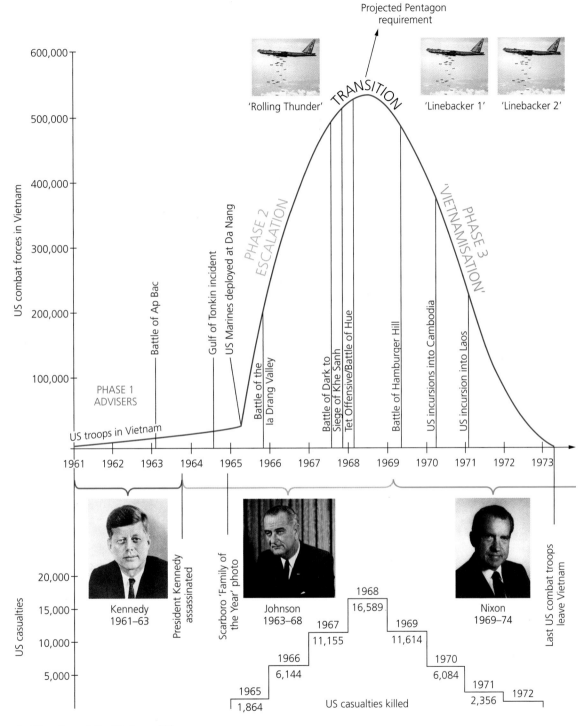

Projected Pentagon requirement

'Rolling Thunder'

TRANSITION

'Linebacker 1'   'Linebacker 2'

PHASE 2
ESCALATION

PHASE 3
'VIETNAMISATION'

US combat forces in Vietnam

600,000

500,000

400,000

300,000

200,000

100,000

PHASE 1
ADVISERS

US troops in Vietnam

Battle of Ap Bac

Gulf of Tonkin incident

US Marines deployed at Da Nang

Battle of the
Ia Drang Valley

Battle of Dark to

Siege of Khe Sanh

Tet Offensive/Battle of Hue

Battle of Hamburger Hill

US incursions into Cambodia

US incursion into Laos

1961   1962   1963   1964   1965   1966   1967   1968   1969   1970   1971   1972   1973

US casualties

President Kennedy assassinated

Scarboro 'Family of the Year' photo

Last US combat troops leave Vietnam

20,000

15,000

10,000

5,000

Kennedy
1961–63

Johnson
1963–68

Nixon
1969–74

1968
16,589

1967
11,155

1969
11,614

1966
6,144

1970
6,084

1965
1,864

1971
2,356

1972

US casualties killed

△ Timeline of the Vietnam War.

A story written in stone

The United States has fought three wars in Asia since 1941 – the Second World War, the Korean War and the war in Vietnam. Over the years these wars have been commemorated in the nation's capital, Washington DC, with stone memorials. Between them they tell the story of America's efforts to stabilise the Far East, from victory through stalemate to defeat. But the memorials also tell another story, the story of the struggle for history, for how those wars should be remembered – or even whether they should be remembered at all.

> For more about this famous event, see the film *Flags of Our Fathers*, directed by Clint Eastwood.

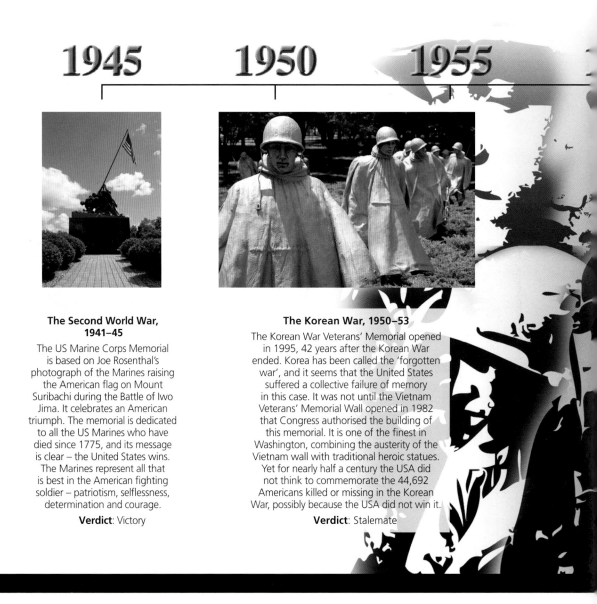

1945   **1950**   **1955**

The Second World War, 1941–45

The US Marine Corps Memorial is based on Joe Rosenthal's photograph of the Marines raising the American flag on Mount Suribachi during the Battle of Iwo Jima. It celebrates an American triumph. The memorial is dedicated to all the US Marines who have died since 1775, and its message is clear – the United States wins. The Marines represent all that is best in the American fighting soldier – patriotism, selflessness, determination and courage.

Verdict: Victory

The Korean War, 1950–53

The Korean War Veterans' Memorial opened in 1995, 42 years after the Korean War ended. Korea has been called the 'forgotten war', and it seems that the United States suffered a collective failure of memory in this case. It was not until the Vietnam Veterans' Memorial Wall opened in 1982 that Congress authorised the building of this memorial. It is one of the finest in Washington, combining the austerity of the Vietnam wall with traditional heroic statues. Yet for nearly half a century the USA did not think to commemorate the 44,692 Americans killed or missing in the Korean War, possibly because the USA did not win it.

Verdict: Stalemate

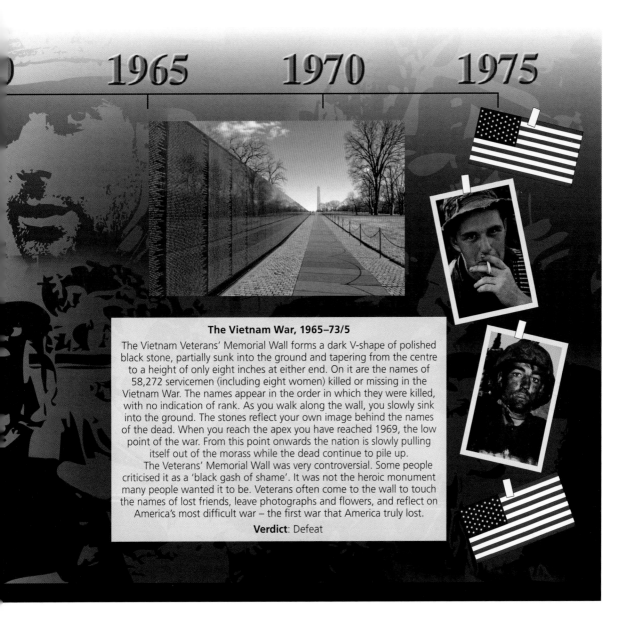

1965   1970   1975

The Vietnam War, 1965–73/5

The Vietnam Veterans' Memorial Wall forms a dark V-shape of polished black stone, partially sunk into the ground and tapering from the centre to a height of only eight inches at either end. On it are the names of 58,272 servicemen (including eight women) killed or missing in the Vietnam War. The names appear in the order in which they were killed, with no indication of rank. As you walk along the wall, you slowly sink into the ground. The stones reflect your own image behind the names of the dead. When you reach the apex you have reached 1969, the low point of the war. From this point onwards the nation is slowly pulling itself out of the morass while the dead continue to pile up.

The Veterans' Memorial Wall was very controversial. Some people criticised it as a 'black gash of shame'. It was not the heroic monument many people wanted it to be. Veterans often come to the wall to touch the names of lost friends, leave photographs and flowers, and reflect on America's most difficult war – the first war that America truly lost.

Verdict: Defeat

Debates and arguments about the Vietnam War

The Vietnam War is still a relatively recent event. There are many people alive today who served in Vietnam. The key decision-makers are now dead, but there are plenty of government records of the war. Vietnam was extensively covered by journalists, photographers and television news; in fact, no other modern war has been reported in as much detail. You might be tempted to assume, therefore, that the 'truth' about Vietnam is plain for all to see. How can people argue about an event that is so well documented, and so recent?

You may be surprised to learn that the Vietnam War has caused more arguments – and more historical debate – than any other modern American event. There are lots of reasons for this. The war was controversial from the moment it began. Within two years, American society was in turmoil about Vietnam. As antiwar protests grew, both the demonstrators and the self-styled patriots felt a real sense of anger and betrayal. The historical debates that grew from this turmoil still reflect this anger. It is precisely because the war is so recent that it is so controversial.

The Vietnam War is still debated not just by historians, but by politicians. America has recently fought wars that bear some similarities to Vietnam. Consequently, argument about Vietnam is laced with a direct contemporary military and political significance. The Vietnam War really wrote the language in which current debates about America's wars are written: the terms 'exit strategies', 'counter-insurgency' and 'collateral damage' all date from Vietnam. In most historical topics, debate is informed not only by the interpretation of evidence but also by the times in which we live. The passage of time changes our perspective and leads to new ways of looking at past events. This is especially true of the Vietnam War.

America has fought three major wars since Vietnam:

- **The Gulf War, 1991** – to throw Iraq's Army out of Kuwait after the invasion of 1990.
- **The Iraq War, 2003** – to overthrow Saddam Hussein and bring about 'regime change' in Iraq.
- **The war in Afghanistan, 2001– 15** – begun following the terrorist attacks on 9/11, to overthrow the Taliban and prevent Al Qaeda from establishing terrorist training bases in Afghanistan.

■ Enquiry Focus: The fault lines of historical debate

Throughout Section 1 of this book you will encounter arguments about the Vietnam War, from broad debates about interpretation to very specific arguments over strategy and tactics. As you work through Chapters 2 to 5, you should make notes on these debates. To help you, wherever there are significant arguments to record, a ✗ symbol appears in the margin. When you get to Chapter 6 these debates will be reviewed to help you to reach your own conclusions about how to interpret the war.

The orthodox view

In the mid-1970s most people agreed that the Vietnam War was a terrible mistake. America had misinterpreted what was happening in Vietnam, and placed too much importance on it. In the early 1960s, American politicians had believed in a 'monolithic' communist threat, with all communist activity orchestrated by the Soviet Union and China. **Détente** with China and Russia proved in the early 1970s that this was not true. In the immediate aftermath of the war there was little debate: writers like David Halberstam and Arthur Schlesinger Jr dominated academic thinking, men who argued that the war was unnecessary and unwinnable. We might call this viewpoint the orthodox consensus.

Example: Extract from *The Arrogance of Power*, by Senator J.W. Fulbright, published in 1966.

Step by step, as it became increasingly clear that the South Vietnamese Army was being defeated, the American commitment increased. The result has been that through a series of limited escalations, each one of which has been more or less compatible with the view that the war was not our war and would have to be won or lost by the South Vietnamese themselves, the war has become our war.

Summary: America got sucked into a quagmire. The communists won because America got bogged down in an unwinnable war.

Détente
President Nixon's policy of driving a wedge between China and the Soviet Union by improving America's relations with both countries.

The revisionist view

The orthodox view was first challenged after the war by US officers who blamed the American Government for not allowing the military to use its power effectively in Vietnam. They complained that they were forced to fight the war with one hand tied behind their backs. They were highly critical of US Government policy for failing to develop realistic plans for achieving American objectives. They particularly blamed President Johnson, his secretary of defence Robert McNamara, and the secretary of state Dean Rusk. They also believed that the so-called liberal press undermined public support through its free reporting of the war. Revisionism then developed into a more general critique of orthodox interpretations.

Example: Extract from *We Were Soldiers Once … and Young*, by Lt Gen Harold Moore and Joseph Galloway, published in 1992.

Johnson decided, against the advice of his military chiefs, that the American escalation in South Vietnam be conducted on the cheap: There would be no mobilisation of reserve and National Guard units, no declaration of a state of emergency that would permit the Army to extend for the duration the enlistments of the best-trained and most experienced soldiers. Instead, the war would be fed by stripping the Army divisions in Europe and the continental United States of their best personnel and materiel, while a river of new draftees, 20,000 of them each month, flowed in to do the shooting and the dying.

Summary: The communists won because the US military was betrayed by political incompetence and liberal defeatism spawned by the news media.

Why should we study America's wars in Asia?

I grew up in America in the 1960s. My friends and I were the young brothers of boys who faced the draft or who actually fought in Vietnam. Our fathers fought in the Second World War, or in Korea. Night after night on television we watched black-and-white news reports about our soldiers fighting in Vietnam. Day by day we saw many of our assumptions about America crumble:

- Our leaders know what they are doing … or do they?
- American soldiers do not commit atrocities … or do they?
- America always wins … or do we?

And year by year the war came closer, until we faced the possibility that we, too, might be sent to Vietnam. The war was in Asia, but by the time the war ended, America had been changed forever.

The Vietnam War had lasting consequences

The Vietnam War has been described as the most important American event of the twentieth century. It divided opinion in America in a way that no other war has done. It forced Americans to make uncomfortable choices, and by doing this, it polarised opinion among Americans about America's policies, its values and its purposes. It inflicted immense damage on America's international prestige. Before Vietnam, America was seen around the world as a force for good. After Vietnam there was lasting suspicion of US policies and attitudes among other nations and peoples.

It is difficult to disentangle Vietnam from the other changes America was experiencing at that time. In the 1960s it was going through a social and cultural revolution. The decade began with Kennedy, pacifist civil rights protests, student tranquillity, acoustic folk music and crew cuts; it ended with Nixon, the Black Panthers, student demonstrations, inner-city riots, assassinations, drugs, long hair and Led Zeppelin. This leads us to a key question that will be explored later: how did the Vietnam War affect the United States?

Why is it difficult to understand these wars today?

Looking at the world today, you might think that America won the Vietnam War. Today the kind of international order that America was seeking in Asia has largely been achieved. Globalisation of the world economy has stabilised the region to a degree Americans in the Cold War would not have thought possible. Communist China has become the workshop of the world; your vacuum cleaner was probably made in China. The trainers on your feet were probably made in Vietnam. Your DVD recorder was probably made in Korea. The Cold War ended over 20 years ago, so communism is no longer the threat it once was. Many people are still alive who served in these wars, but already it takes a leap of the imagination to understand what they went through, and why the wars were fought.

What does the future hold for Southeast Asia?

As I write this, North Korea is threatening its neighbours with nuclear weapons. North Korea is the last Stalinist communist country left in the world. It has recently developed nuclear weapons and missiles that it claims are capable of hitting American targets in the Pacific. By the time you read this, its missiles will probably be able to reach the United States. If North Korea attacks the South, the Americans will once again find themselves at war with a communist country in Asia.

The United States recently announced its intention to shift 60 per cent of its naval forces to the Pacific Ocean. This has nothing to do with the current Korean crisis: it is a response to the growing importance of Pacific Rim countries to the world economy. An American strategist recently said, 'China should and will take note. The United States is and will remain a Pacific power, even more so in this century than in the last.' Most analysts agree that communist China is set to become a Pacific superpower in the first half of this century – which means that, by the time you are my age, China will be the greatest economic and military threat to the United States. To understand what is happening in Asia, people will need to know how the rise of communist China led America to fight wars in Korea and Vietnam. George Santayana, a Spanish-American philosopher, once said, 'Those who cannot remember the past are condemned to repeat it.' Watch this space!

History books usually tell their stories in chronological order – the order in which things really happened. To understand cause and effect, the causes and consequences of events, this is usually the right thing to do. This book, however, takes a different approach. It starts with the Vietnam War, which is likely to be the main interest of the students studying this subject. It tries to recreate the learning process that Americans had to go through during this difficult and divisive war, a war that seemed so simple but turned out to be so complex. As America learned more about the origins of this war, so you will go back in time to pick up the threads of Vietnam, then back to the Second World War and Korea to put Vietnam in perspective.

Vietnam → Vietnam's origins → The Second World War → The Korean War

America, communism and the Cold War: The context for the Vietnam War

The communist view of history

Karl Marx is regarded as the founding father of the communist movement – so communism is often called Marxism. Karl Marx was a German-born philosopher who lived much of his life in nineteenth-century England. He travelled through the great northern industrial cities observing the poverty of the working class (proletariat). He thought the owners of the mills and the mines, whom he called capitalists, exploited their workers.

Marx argued that all history is explained by the struggle between classes – rich vs. poor, lord vs. vassal, landlord vs. peasant, the powerful vs. the weak. Class struggle was the engine of history, the driving force that moved history forward. He thought that human history was progressive, moving towards a better future through a series of violent confrontations between classes. He called these violent confrontations revolutions.

△ Karl Marx, 1818–83.

'BOURGEOIS' REVOLUTION e.g. French Revolution, 1789	'COMMUNIST' REVOLUTION e.g. Bolshevik Revolution, 1917	
MEDIEVAL FEUDALISM	**MODERN CAPITALISM**	**FUTURE COMMUNISM**
• Governed by kings • Land is the source of wealth • The aristocracy owns the land • Landlord vs. peasant (class struggle)	• Governed by parliaments elected by the bourgeoisie • Industry is the source of wealth • Capitalists own the industry • Capitalist vs. worker (class struggle)	• Government is unnecessary • Industry is the source of wealth • Industry owned by all the people in common, no such thing as property • Harmonious society (no class struggle)

> 'The history of all hitherto existing societies is the history of class struggle.'
>
> Karl Marx,
> *The Communist Manifesto*, 1848

◁ **Revolutionary stages.**

Marx believed this process was inevitable because capitalism bore the seeds of its own destruction. The more industrial a country became, the larger its working class. Sooner or later the workers would get so fed up with their condition that they would rise up and overthrow the **bourgeoisie**. Communist revolutions would succeed first in the most industrially advanced countries – Britain, Germany and America.

ARVN
The South Vietnamese Army.

The Cold War: Context for the Vietnam War

The Vietnam War only makes sense if viewed in the **Cold War** context. It is only because, at that time, Vietnam was part of a global conflict that the US Government felt forced to commit itself to South Vietnam. Once made, the commitment itself became the main point: the United States could not abandon South Vietnam because this would raise serious doubts elsewhere about the value of American promises to fight to prevent the spread of communism. In Asia the 'domino theory' dominated American thinking about the threat posed by communism (see the diagram on page 65).

Cold War
The global confrontation between the Soviet Union and the United States and their allies from 1945 to 1990.

America's Cold War policy – containment

At the present time in world history, nearly every nation must choose between alternative ways of life. The choice is too often not a free one … I believe that we must help free peoples to work out their own futures in their own way.
The Truman Doctrine, 1947

Let every nation know, whether it wishes us well or ill, that we shall pay any price, bear any burden, meet any hardship, support any friend, oppose any foe, to assure the survival and the success of Liberty.
Kennedy's Inaugural Address, 1961

Why are we in South Vietnam? We are there because we have a promise to keep. Since 1954 every American president has offered support to the people of South Vietnam. We have helped to build, and we have helped to defend. Thus over many years we have made a national pledge to help South Vietnam defend its independence. And I intend to keep that promise … We are also there to strengthen world order. Around the globe, from Berlin to Thailand, are people whose wellbeing rests, in part, on the belief that they can count on us if they are attacked.
Johnson's speech at Johns Hopkins University, 1965

Ho Chi Minh

Every communist revolution has its revolutionary leader: Lenin in Russia; Castro in Cuba; Mao Zedong in China. In Vietnam the leader of the revolution was Ho Chi Minh. He was born in Vietnam, a French colony, in 1890, and attended a French school in the ancient imperial capital city of Hue. In 1911 he got a job on a French liner that took him to New York, where he worked in a hotel for a year. During the First World War he lived in America and England, where he supported Chelsea FC! He was obviously a well-educated, well-travelled man (even if he knew nothing about football).

Between 1919 and 1923 he lived in France, where he joined the French Socialist Party. It was an exciting time. In Russia the Bolsheviks had just seized power. Germany, too, was in political turmoil. It looked as if communism was the way of the future. In 1920 Ho Chi Minh became a founder member of the French Communist Party, denouncing French colonialism in Vietnam. During the Paris Peace Conference he petitioned President Woodrow Wilson of America to use his influence to help give Vietnam its independence from France. The failure of these efforts made him even more determined to achieve independence for Vietnam, and made him a nationalist hero in his home country. He was both a communist and a patriot.

In 1923 Ho Chi Minh went to Moscow to work for the **Comintern** and learn more about revolutions at first hand. Russian communism at this time was caught up in the power struggle between Stalin and Trotsky after Lenin's death. When Stalin emerged triumphant, he ordered the Communist Party in Indochina to break off relations with the nationalist middle classes and to focus on the (almost non-existent) proletariat. Instead, Ho Chi Minh remained loyal to Lenin's ideas. In a paper called *Imperialism: The Highest Form of Capitalism* Lenin had argued that industrial, imperialist countries like Britain and France exploited their colonies to maintain a higher standard of living among their industrial workers. If these colonies could revolt, the peasants in these colonies could be freed from exploitation, and it would also hasten the coming of revolutions in the industrial nations. To bring this about, it was necessary for the peasants to make common cause with the 'national bourgeoisie' – middle-class nationalists demanding independence – instead of fighting them. Ho Chi Minh found these ideas very attractive and thought he might be able to apply them in his own country.

The Second World War brought him back to Vietnam, which the Japanese occupied in 1940 with the rest of French Indochina. In 1941 he became the political leader of the Viet Minh, a communist guerrilla force fighting against the Japanese. From then on Ho Chi Minh led the Viet Minh through a series of three wars, against the Japanese, the French and – finally – the Americans. He died in 1969 – still fighting.

△ Ho Chi Minh, 1890–1969.

Comintern
The Communist International, set up after the Russian Revolution to promote communist revolutions in other countries.

How did Ho Chi Minh apply communist theory in Vietnam?

Ho Chi Minh's main contribution to the communist victory in Vietnam was both ideological and practical. In a peasant society like Vietnam classic Marxist theory would not work. Capitalism was not yet fully developed, and therefore there was no large proletariat. Ho Chi Minh's approach to the problem was pragmatic: communism could not be built in Vietnam as long as the country was in the hands of a foreign power. He therefore compromised with middle-class nationalists in order to broaden his base of support. This enabled his movement to sustain the high casualties suffered during the long struggle against the French, the Americans and the regime in South Vietnam.

Ho Chi Minh also borrowed ideas from communist China, where Mao Zedong showed that a peasant revolution could go straight from feudalism to socialism. The key to his success was land reform, seizing land from feudal overlords. The situation in Vietnam was similar to that in China.

The ideological debt that Ho Chi Minh owed to Lenin and to Mao was important because it showed that he placed his country's independence above loyalty to Stalin's regime in Russia. In other words, he was more a nationalist than a communist, though he did believe that communism offered his countrymen a new beginning. He also believed that Vietnam could play a part in a great worldwide revolution: its independence would hasten changes in France, which would be beneficial to the French working classes.

Ho Chi Minh's thinking was also important because it showed that the United States was not correct to assume that all communists were simply following orders from Moscow. The American war in Vietnam was based on this assumption. The discovery that it was not true came too late to prevent America getting involved in this devastating and disastrous war.

COMMUNIST 'PEASANT' REVOLUTION

MEDIEVAL FEUDALISM

MODERN CAPITALISM

FUTURE COMMUNISM AND NATIONAL INDEPENDENCE

2 Did the USA defeat itself in the Vietnam War?

A soap opera

In 1965 my school took part in a charity drive to help the people of South Vietnam. The Government was looking for a gift that American children could easily provide. It settled on soap: soap was inexpensive, easy to package, and it would not spoil on the long trip to Southeast Asia. The word went out; we asked our mothers for a bar of soap, and a few days later we turned up at school carrying our bars of Camay, Lifebuoy and Zest. What the long-suffering people of Vietnam needed, apparently, was a good hot bath.

Meanwhile the war was getting dirty. As American troops poured into South Vietnam, the Viet Cong went to ground, digging underground bunkers. At Cu Chi, near Saigon, the American 25th Infantry Division settled into a large base near the area known as the Iron Triangle. Unknown at first to the Americans, the 25th Division's base was on top of an enormous Viet Cong tunnel complex.

The Army tried to flush out the Viet Cong (VC); brave soldiers known as tunnel rats crawled into the tunnels carrying pistols, hand grenades and flashlights and engaged the VC in hand-to-hand fighting. A lot of the tunnel rats were killed. Then the Army tried something else. German Shepherd dogs were trained to go into the tunnels and attack the Viet Cong. At first the method worked well, but the VC found a way to prevent these attacks. They washed in American soap. The dogs would not attack people who smelled like Americans.

Eventually the Army bulldozed the tunnels, burying many Viet Cong alive. Today the tunnels of Cu Chi are a tourist attraction, reconstructed to give the impression that the Americans never destroyed them. But the ingenuity of the Viet Cong, and the way they used our soap to defeat the Army's dogs, suggests that in some respects the American war effort in Vietnam was self-defeating.

Why are we starting this book at the end of the story? I am trying to recreate for you the experience that we Americans shared. Most of us did not know why the war started, and did not take much notice until we started to lose it. Then it all came out, and the history of the war became of vital importance.

Building a hypothesis

The idea that the Americans defeated themselves in Vietnam has a much wider provenance than a simple story about bars of soap. In 2010 an American veteran, Karl Marlantes, published a novel based on his experiences as a US Marine. In his novel, the Marines fortify a position on a hilltop called Matterhorn. They dig the bunkers and work out all the best positions, with overlapping fields of fire to make the mountain impregnable – and then they are ordered to abandon it. The North Vietnamese then occupy Matterhorn and the Marines are ordered to take it back, which they do, with considerable loss. *Matterhorn* is a work of fiction, but it is symbolic of Marlantes' experience of the war. It also contains references to other aspects of the war with a basis in fact – for example, the way the US Air Force dropped **Agent Orange** on its own troops; racial tension undermining the combat effectiveness of American units; and incidents of 'fragging', where Americans murdered their own officers. The Marine Corps alone had 43 fragging incidents during the Vietnam War.

The same theme recurs in Vietnam War films. Oliver Stone, a Vietnam War veteran, directed *Platoon,* in which the platoon is virtually destroyed by in-fighting between two sergeants with different views on how the war should be fought.

Apart from anecdotes, fiction and Hollywood movies, have any professional historians argued that the American war effort was self-defeating? The answer is yes. Neal Sheehan covered the war as a journalist from the early 1960s, and in 1988 he published his history, *A Bright Shining Lie.* His thesis was that American advisors warned the US Government that the war was going badly but that the Government did not listen. In 2007 Mark Moyar published *Triumph Forsaken: The Vietnam War, 1954–1965* in which he argued that America made many mistakes. These included its support for the military coup that overthrew the first president of South Vietnam, Ngo Dinh Diem, in 1963.

Agent Orange
A chemical used by the Americans to kill plants in order to reveal enemy troop movements. It is now known to have caused cancer in many soldiers and civilians who were exposed to it.

For an outline of the main events, see the timeline of the Vietnam War on page 9.

■ Enquiry Focus: Did the USA defeat itself in the Vietnam War?

The idea that America defeated itself in Vietnam is attractive because it would explain how a poor Third World country defeated the world's mightiest superpower. However, in seeking our own explanation for the communist victory in Vietnam, we need to place the American war effort in a wider context. The Vietnam War was not just between America and North Vietnam. Many countries were involved.

Therefore we need to consider not only what the Americans did wrong, but also what the communists did right, and whether the weakness of South Vietnam as a country meant that the USA could not have won the war, whatever it did.

Your aim in this enquiry is to construct a clear, well-structured and detailed explanation of why, in your opinion, the Americans lost the war. To help you this chapter analyses, in turn, the part played by each of the main three countries – the USA, South Vietnam and North Vietnam – in deciding the outcome of the war. As you read about each of these countries, you need to collect ideas and information to go in each of their three folders. At the end of the enquiry you will be able to use the ideas and information in the three folders to explain why, in your opinion, the Americans lost the war.

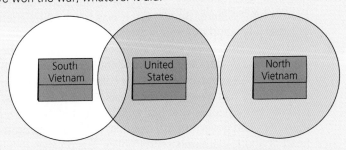

South Vietnam: Was America shackled to a corpse?

■ Add notes to your folder on South Vietnam explaining what each of these tells us about the strengths and weaknesses of South Vietnam during the war:

- the Buddhist crisis of 1963
- the coup d'etat that overthrew President Diem in 1963 and the subsequent instability of South Vietnam's Government
- the impact of American economic aid and the 'hearts and minds' programme
- the attitude of South Vietnamese officers to fighting the Viet Cong
- the Strategic Hamlets programme – did it do more harm than good?

△ Thich Quang Duc's self-immolation.

The man in this photograph is Thich Quang Duc, a Buddhist monk. On 11 June 1963 he arrived in a procession of monks at a road junction in Saigon. Stepping out of an old car, he sat down in the middle of the junction and began to meditate. Another monk produced a can of petrol and poured it over Thich Quang Duc's head. Duc calmly said a prayer, struck a match and dropped it on himself. His body erupted into a grotesque fireball in which Duc rocked back and forth in silence. Finally his body fell to the ground, where it continued to burn. The whole incident was photographed and filmed.

Thich Quang Duc's decision to commit suicide in so horrible and public a manner was taken in the context of the 'Buddhist crisis' of 1963. The president of South Vietnam, Ngo Dinh Diem, was a Catholic but there was more at stake than religion. Catholicism represented the whole French way of life, the product of a century of French colonialism. However, the majority of the population were Buddhists. As people protested against Diem's Government, they looked to the monks for political and moral leadership. In May 1963 President Diem ordered his army to break up Buddhist demonstrations, leading to the deaths of several monks. Thich Quang Duc's suicide was a protest against Diem's repression of Buddhism. It was followed by a temporary imposition of martial law and numerous arrests.

The Buddhist crisis was a symptom of a much deeper problem. Diem was the first leader of an independent South Vietnam. But to many people he still represented foreign colonialism, French or American. His Government had a very narrow basis of support, consisting largely of Catholics and people who had collaborated with the French. Several family members had government positions, including his brother Ngo Dinh Nhu, head of South Vietnam's secret police. His policies defended the economic and social status quo, the Catholic minority, landowners and capitalists. It was the Army, not democracy, that held Diem's Government in place. He felt threatened by any move to give more power to the people, the majority of whom were Buddhists. To many people it seemed that nothing had really changed since independence. As Diem's position deteriorated, his regime became more repressive.

The United States found this deeply embarrassing. America was defending South Vietnam in the name of freedom and democracy as part of its global strategy to contain the spread of communism. To succeed, it needed to create a viable government in the South, one that had enough support to survive the many threats it faced. America had a strategy to achieve this:

1. Economic aid.
The US Agency for International Development (USAID) was an American agency set up by President Kennedy in 1961. Walt Rostow (Kennedy's deputy assistant for national security) persuaded Kennedy that the most effective way to stop the spread of communism was to encourage economic development. It was aimed specifically at the many undeveloped nations gaining independence in the 1950s and early 1960s, including South Vietnam.

America's aim – to strengthen South Vietnam.

2. Military advice.
In February 1962 President Kennedy sent General Paul Harkins to Vietnam as head of a new Military Assistance Command, Vietnam (MACV) that placed American officers alongside their South Vietnamese counterparts to teach them the art of war. He also created the Special Forces (Green Berets) as a special counter-insurgency force, to fight back against communist guerrillas.

3. Political and social reform.
Something had to be done to make Ngo Dinh Diem's Government more popular. For example, tackling the corruption endemic to the South Vietnamese Government; inviting more Buddhists and members of other sects to take part in government; social changes to appeal to the peasantry and split them off from the communists.

The effectiveness of the US strategies in South Vietnam

Economic failure: Aid undermined by corruption

American economic aid flowed into South Vietnam from 1954 until South Vietnam's defeat in 1975. In the 1960s this was called the 'hearts and minds' programme, aimed at showing the South Vietnamese people that American friendship brought real benefits – schools, medicine, food, fresh water – and soap. But from the earliest days there were signs that the policy was misconceived. Much of the aid sent by the USA was siphoned off and sold by corrupt government officials.

In his book *A Bright Shining Lie*, Neil Sheehan told a story that illustrated the problem. John Paul Vann and Daniel Ellsberg were two American government officials involved in the aid programme. In one village they set about repairing the village school, bringing in blackboards and chalk, textbooks and maps, and materials to strengthen the roof and make it waterproof. When a local Vietnamese official demanded payment for these materials, the Americans refused. The next thing they knew, the South Vietnamese Air Force bombed the village and the school was destroyed, on the grounds that the villagers were VC. The bombing raid was ordered by the local official to punish the Americans for their refusal to pay him off.

Military failure: The Battle of Ap Bac

ARVN
The South Vietnamese Army.

Ultimately, the reason America committed its own combat forces to the war in Vietnam was because it came to realise that the **ARVN** was incapable of winning it. This fact was brought home by the Battle of Ap Bac in January 1963.

John Paul Vann's job was to teach the ARVN how to fight the Viet Cong. The problem was that the VC always managed to escape South Vietnamese attacks. Vann showed his fellow officers that a pincer movement could drive the VC from their strongholds, herding them in one direction. American helicopters could then drop soldiers in their line of flight to close the route of escape. But time and again, some ARVN officer failed to press home his attack, giving the VC a way out. It became clear that many ARVN officers feared direct conflict with the Viet Cong, or thought that if their own troops suffered casualties, they would lose face with President Diem. They often lied about how many enemy soldiers they killed, and sometimes they used American intelligence reports to avoid contact with the Viet Cong.

▽ **The American tactic for defeating the Viet Cong in small battles.**

American efforts to teach the ARVN how to defeat the Viet Cong focused on the use of helicopters to block their escape.

Phase ① — ARVN forces attack from three sides — Enemy-held village

Phase ② — Viet Cong flee in the only direction possible

Phase ③ — American helicopters land ARVN troops and block the escape

On 2 January 1963 American soldiers died because the ARVN would not fight. It happened near the village of Ap Bac, held by the Viet Cong, whose forces occupied a tree line at one end of the village. An American helicopter was shot down when its pilot misjudged the landing site. With Americans pinned down in the open, another helicopter sent to rescue them was also shot down. Circling overhead in a spotter plane, Vann tried to persuade waiting South Vietnamese troops in armoured vehicles to go to their rescue. The result was a fiasco: the ARVN refused to fight, and several Americans were killed. It was the first time the Viet Cong had stood their ground and won. It raised serious doubts about the ability of South Vietnam's forces to fight their own battles.

Social failure: The 'Strategic Hamlets' programme

The failure of social reform to prop up the South Vietnamese Government was illustrated by the policy of Strategic Hamlets. Encouraged by the Americans, Diem's Government evicted peasants from their ancestral homes to live in new fortified villages. The idea was to remove them from the influence of communist infiltrators, but the policy backfired. Weapons distributed to the strategic hamlets found their way into the hands of the

Viet Cong. The policy also revealed a profound insensitivity to the beliefs and values of the peasants themselves, who worshipped the ancestors whose spirits they believed inhabited their ancient homes. It is not surprising that many peasants came to support the Viet Cong.

Political failure: The instability of South Vietnamese politics

Most of the issues described above were the problems of the Government of Ngo Dinh Diem, but the following presidents were not much better. In November 1963 Diem was overthrown and murdered in a military coup encouraged by the CIA. This was followed by a series of military coups. Between November 1963 and June 1965 South Vietnam had seven presidents, often holding power for no more than a few weeks.

In his memoirs Philip Caputo, a US Marine, described the odd situation in which he and his fellow Marines found themselves in late 1965. A civil war had broken out in Danang between rival military leaders. The Marines were dug in on a hill defending the airfield from the communist guerrillas to the west. Behind them, to the east, South Vietnamese aircraft were bombing and strafing South Vietnamese troops. It seemed obvious to many American soldiers that the regime they were defending was doomed.

> I don't want to hear any more about this goddamned coup shit.
>
> President Johnson

Was America shackled to a corpse?

It is tempting to conclude that South Vietnam was a failing state that lost the support of many of its own people and that the Americans lost the war because they backed a loser. If South Vietnam had enjoyed the determination, sacrifice, courage and confidence of the North Vietnamese, it might not have lost. There are two problems with this analysis, however.

Firstly, not all historians agree that South Vietnam was a lost cause. There is evidence that some progress was made in the reforms America wanted. In his book *Triumph Forsaken* (2006), Mark Moyar argued that, with the support of American advisers, President Ngo Dinh Diem was winning the war before he was assassinated in 1963. The last president of South Vietnam, Nguyen Van Thieu, managed to govern for ten years until the country fell in 1975. Furthermore, some South Vietnamese Army units were dedicated troops prepared to stand and fight. By 1969 South Vietnam had an army of 850,000 soldiers, and Nixon's Vietnamisation programme had ensured that they were well equipped. Perhaps if the war had been fought differently, reforms might have had time to take root and make South Vietnam stronger.

Secondly, even if it was true that South Vietnam was doomed, it was a truth that may not have been visible when the key decisions were made. During the Cold War America supported many countries whose governments were corrupt, dictatorial and unpopular. Most of them did not fall to communism. Maybe there was no reason, at the outset, to think that South Vietnam would turn out differently.

---

1 Use the notes in your folder to identify three major ways in which the South Vietnamese contributed to the defeat of the USA.

2 Did the condition of South Vietnam make the defeat of the USA:
   a) certain
   b) probable
   c) possible?
   Explain your choice.

25

The communist war effort

■ Add notes to your folder on North Vietnam explaining what each of these tells us about the strengths and weaknesses of the communist war effort:

- North Vietnam's strategy
- the tactics used by North Vietnam and the National Liberation Front (NLF)
- the way the communists appealed to the 'hearts and minds' of the South Vietnamese peasants
- the brutality used by communist forces
- support for North Vietnam from the Soviet Union and China.

The United States was the most powerful enemy the Vietnamese communists faced, far more powerful than the Japanese or the French had been. How did Ho Chi Minh, General Giap and other communist leaders fight the Americans?

We have already seen how Ho Chi Minh applied communist theory to the Vietnam War. He realised that the proletariat in Indochina was too small to form an exclusive basis for revolution, so he urged the Vietnamese Communist Party to work together with the bourgeoisie, the nationalist bourgeoisie and the peasants. He therefore appealed to nationalists of all persuasions.

Under his leadership Vietnam's independence and its communist future were blended into one seemingly inescapable destiny. The communists were seen as the only legitimate nationalist force. In the chaos of back-alley restaurants, laundries and money-lenders that formed Vietnam's budding entrepreneurial class, nationalism forged an alliance with communists seeking to take land from the old ex-colonial landlords and distribute it to the peasants.

Communism also helped the North Vietnamese Army (NVA) and the Viet Cong to overcome one of the most crippling aspects of South Vietnam's war effort – the compulsion to save face. Among the communists, the ideological imperative of the class war was as powerful as local culture. In South Vietnam evasion and self-deception were endemic. In North Vietnam counter-revolutionary activity was punishable by re-education or death.

Strategy

It is important to understand that the communist war effort consisted of two parts:

■ North of the demilitarised zone (DMZ; see map on page 2), communist North Vietnam provided the firepower, the conventional army and the political direction of the war. The NVA could invade South Vietnam, either across the DMZ or at any point along the Ho Chi Minh Trail.

■ In South Vietnam itself there was the National Liberation Front (NLF). Its soldiers were the Viet Cong (VC), a guerrilla force raised from indigenous communist rebels. Aided and supplied by the NVA, the VC fought on home territory, taking advantage of their knowledge of local terrain.

The combination of these forces gave the communists great flexibility. Fighting the Americans and the South Vietnamese Army (ARVN) the communists adopted the same three-part strategy they used successfully against the French:

Phase 1: building a secure base beyond the reach of the enemy's main force. During the American war the whole of North Vietnam served this purpose, as the Americans had no intention of invading the North.

Phase 2: a long period of guerrilla warfare, supported by NVA incursions. Guerrilla warfare enabled small numbers of guerrillas to pin down larger numbers of American and South Vietnamese troops. Americans on combat patrols never knew when they might trigger a hand grenade, step on **punji sticks**, walk into an ambush or detonate a landmine. The Viet Cong blended into the local population and blurred the distinction between combatants and civilians. This encouraged the Americans to kill innocent people, which fuelled anti-American feeling and ensured replacements for VC casualties.

Phase 3: the end-game. Guerrilla tactics gave way to large-scale conventional battles led by the NVA, accompanied by a general VC offensive in both the countryside and planned uprisings in the cities. The siege of Khe Sanh, the battle for Hue and the Tet Offensive in 1968 were part of a premature attempt to move the war into a third, decisive phase. But other battles followed. In 1972 the NVA launched its Easter Offensive resulting in large-scale battles at Quang Tri in the north, An Loc in the south and Kontum in the Central Highlands. In March 1974, after the Americans left, the NVA launched a general offensive that led to the collapse and defeat of South Vietnam.

Punji sticks
A booby trap consisting of sharp stakes smeared with human excrement and hidden in a camouflaged pit. The injuries they inflicted usually became infected.

△ American soldiers searching the trees for snipers, Phuoc Vinh, 1967.

Tactics

The Battle of the Ia Drang Valley (1965) taught the North Vietnamese an important tactical lesson. To minimise the effect of American firepower, communist troops were taught to 'cling to the belt' of the Americans. By closing with American forces and fighting hand-to-hand, the communists could prevent the USA from unleashing the full force of its artillery, napalm and other high-impact weapons. This became the general tactic of regular NVA forces, alongside the hit-and-run tactics of the VC guerrillas.

Hearts and minds

The communists tried hard to win over support from the peasantry. Their forces were issued with a series of orders about how to behave towards the peasants. These included:

- not to damage the land and crops or spoil the houses and belongings of the people
- not to buy or borrow what the people are not willing to sell or lend
- never to break their word
- not to do or say anything likely to make people believe that they held the people in contempt
- to help them in their daily work (harvesting, fetching firewood, carrying water, etc.).

This discipline and friendliness often contrasted with the behaviour of ARVN forces, who often suspected peasants of being communist sympathisers and treated them accordingly.

Brutality

There is a telling scene in the 1979 Hollywood film *Apocalypse Now*. A renegade American officer, Colonel Kurtz, is explaining why he has turned to outright savagery in his war against the communists. In the words of another American, Kurtz has gone insane. In self-defence, Kurtz tells a story. He recounts how he and his unit went to a Vietnamese village and inoculated the children against polio. When they left, the Viet Cong went into the village and murdered all the children to show the peasants that there was nothing to be gained from American support.

There is no evidence at all that such an event actually happened in Vietnam. What is interesting is that American cinema audiences in the 1970s were prepared to believe that these events were real. It tells us that many Americans thought the Viet Cong were utterly ideologically ruthless – and, of course, it tells us that Kurtz thought the VC were right to do this. As he says in the film, 'Horror and moral terror are your friends.' His conclusion is that the Americans are losing the war because they are not as brutal as the communists.

Were the communists more brutal than the Americans? How can we gauge brutality in a war? One of the problems facing historians is that so much of the evidence about war crimes is based on hearsay. It is important, therefore, to stick to properly documented evidence. When the North Vietnamese Army captured Hue in 1968, political officers murdered anyone who had served the South Vietnamese regime: when they retook the city, the Americans found over 4,000 bodies in mass graves. Assassinations were commonplace. The Americans, too, used assassination during the Phoenix programme in the early 1970s to eliminate Viet Cong cadres in rural villages.

What conclusions can we draw about this aspect of the war? The South Vietnamese were terrified of the communists. When South Vietnam fell to the North in 1975, people desperate to avoid retribution besieged the American Embassy. It is a commonplace observation that America lost its moral compass in Vietnam, but we should remember that American forces represented an open society and operated in the full glare of publicity, whereas communist forces faced no such condemnation for their actions. It was doubly important, therefore, for the Americans to adhere strictly to international law. Sometimes they did not. If communist brutality helped the communists to win, American brutality helped America to lose. This democratic conundrum still haunts American forces today in other wars.

Support from the Soviet Union and China

The Vietnam War was a war by proxy between the USA and the main communist powers. North Vietnam relied on weapons and ammunition imported from its communist mentors to the north. American air power mined the port of Haiphong and repeatedly tried to destroy the bridges over which these supplies entered North Vietnam, but the supplies got through. Furthermore, **SAM missiles** manned by Soviet soldiers were used to defend North Vietnam against American bombers. It was one of the few places in the Cold War where Soviet and American forces clashed directly.

SAM missiles
Soviet surface-to-air missiles.

◁ North Vietnamese tanks smash their way into the grounds of South Vietnam's presidential palace in Saigon, at the end of the war, 30 April 1975.

■ It is time to draw some conclusions about the communist war effort. What should we place in the North Vietnam folder? Again, it is up to you to decide how important this was to America's defeat, and it is an important question. Did the communists really beat the Americans? Or is this a war that America could have won if it had played its cards right? Whatever you decide, there are some things you need to take into consideration:

- Ho Chi Minh's leadership. How did he adapt Marxist theory to the circumstances that existed in Vietnam? How did this help the communists?

- What was the strategy used by North Vietnam?
- What tactics were used by:

  a) the North Vietnamese Army?

  b) the Viet Cong?

- How far did the communists go to win the support of the South Vietnamese people, especially the peasantry?

- How ruthless were the communists in the way they fought?

America in Vietnam: A chained eagle?

One of the most common claims made by American Vietnam veterans is that the United States never used the power available to it. America was like a chained eagle – ready and willing to fight, but unable to use its full array of weapons or attack the enemy in their own country. It is a view that has become more common in recent years. The logical reverse of the coin is that the USA would have won if the military had been given a free hand. The blame, then, is levelled at the politicians who hamstrung the military and prevented the US Army from fulfilling its mission, especially President Johnson. How convincing is this view?

Before you can answer this question, you need to be clear about the mission itself. What, exactly, was America trying to achieve in Vietnam? In most of the wars you will have studied, the aim was the unconditional surrender of the enemy nation – Germany in 1918 and Germany and Japan in 1945. In Vietnam this was not so. America's aims in Vietnam were:

△ The US Veterans' Prisoner of War Silver Dollar, 1994, shows a chained eagle breaking free through a circle of barbed wire.

- to guarantee the independence of South Vietnam
- to prevent a communist take-over in South Vietnam
- to prevent communism spreading from Vietnam to other countries in Southeast Asia – Laos and Cambodia, Thailand, Burma, Malaysia – the so-called 'domino effect'.

In Vietnam the Americans were hoping to repeat their success in Korea, where a communist invasion was halted and a border stabilised around a demilitarised zone. But America had made the mistake in 1950 of invading North Korea during the fighting, provoking Chinese intervention and making the war much bigger. This would not happen in Vietnam; the president ruled out an invasion of the North. So America was fighting a defensive war aimed at persuading North Vietnam to negotiate and leave South Vietnam intact.

■ Add notes to your folder on the United States explaining what each of these tells us about the strengths and weaknesses of the American war effort. In each case you should indicate whether the failure of each of these strategies was due to political interference – 'chained eagle' syndrome:

- the hearts and minds programme
- the bombing of North Vietnam
- military strategy before 1968
- military strategy after 1968.

Remember that for each point you are trying to decide whether America was really using all the power available to it, or whether political considerations tied the hands of the US military.

The hearts and minds campaign

In 1976 I attended a university seminar that brought together several American officers fresh from Vietnam. One of the officers who spoke was involved in the **hearts and minds** programme. He explained the failure of the programme in the following terms. An American platoon approaches a Vietnamese village and is fired upon. The platoon commander is ordered to clear the village of enemy soldiers, and therefore faces a dilemma. He has at his disposal an unbelievable amount of firepower – mortars, artillery, fighter-bombers, possibly even B-52 strikes, more than enough firepower to wipe the village off the map. If he chooses old-fashioned house-to-house infantry fighting, he knows his platoon will suffer casualties. The temptation, then, is to call in the firepower and spare his men. But by doing so, he is losing the hearts and minds of the people he has come to save – the Vietnamese peasants. In the famous words of another American officer, 'We had to destroy the village in order to save it.'

It could be argued, therefore, that the hearts and minds programme was incompatible with practical military necessity. A poorer country than the United States might have forced its officers to clear such villages with foot patrols, running the risk of higher casualties but less likely to alienate the local population. Western armies seem to have learned this lesson from Vietnam – during the recent war in Afghanistan, a much more sensitive approach was adopted by American and British forces, at great risk to themselves. But Vietnam was America's first experience of this kind of warfare, and American troops had all the firepower they could ask for. It helped them to win battles, but it tended to undermine the war's political objective.

In this sense, therefore, the failure of hearts and minds contradicts the idea that America was a chained eagle, because American firepower undermined the efficacy of the programme. It is doubtful whether hearts and minds could ever have worked, given the agricultural nature of the Vietnamese economy. Vietnam was not a country on the brink of an industrial revolution, and its people were unlikely to choose the benefits of mass consumerism over the clear goals of national independence and reunification.

Hearts and minds
A programme of economic aid to South Vietnam, aimed at persuading the people to support the South Vietnamese Government and its American sponsors. It was part of a larger programme begun under President Kennedy to encourage economic growth in Third World countries, thereby making communism less attractive in the under-developed world.

Let this session of Congress be known as the session—which declared all-out war on human poverty."
—*PRESIDENT JOHNSON, JANUARY 8, 1964*

△ Cartoon from the *Evening Standard*, 1 December 1965, highlighting the American dilemma.

The bombing of North Vietnam

Using American air power to bomb North Vietnam lay at the heart of America's strategy after 1964. The chief proponent of the bombing campaign was Walt W. Rostow, a foreign policy advisor to both Kennedy and Johnson. The best way to fight communism in peacetime, he said, was to help Third World countries achieve 'take-off' towards prosperity by giving them aid. During a war, however, the flip side of the coin was bombing; faced with the destruction of his economic base, Ho Chi Minh would surely abandon his support for the NLF. In the early 1960s Rostow was sidelined by President Kennedy, who rejected Rostow's advocacy of bombing because the communists might interpret it as an act of desperation. The image of the world's greatest superpower bombing a poor Third World country to oblivion would not, he thought, sit well alongside his support for Third World aid and concern for the world's poor. It was also suggested that strategic bombing would not work, because North Vietnam's motives (reunification and an NLF victory in the South) would not be affected by any physical damage inflicted on it by American planes. In retrospect, since it failed, it seems clear that Kennedy was right to reject the bombing strategy, and this became a central theme of the orthodox view of the war.

After Kennedy's assassination Rostow's ideas gained Johnson's support and became the central doctrine of America's war effort. The Americans called this first bombing campaign 'Operation Rolling Thunder'. Rolling Thunder began in March 1965 and lasted for three years. It became the heaviest strategic bombing campaign in history, dropping over 864,000 tons of bombs on North Vietnam by the end of 1967. By contrast, during the Second World War the United States dropped 623,418 tons of bombs on Germany and around 150,000 tons on Japan.

Joint Chiefs of Staff
The heads of the US Army, Air Force and Navy (which includes the Marines).

President Johnson's decision to bomb North Vietnam was controversial in itself, for the same reasons that Kennedy had rejected it. It was also controversial because of the way that he chose to do it. The **Joint Chiefs of Staff** wanted an all-out bombing campaign that would bring North Vietnam to its knees, quickly. To achieve this they drew up a list of targets that would, in the words of General Curtis LeMay, bomb North Vietnam 'back to the Stone Age'. Johnson rejected their advice in favour of Rostow's own thesis of gradualism. By holding targets of greater strategic value in reserve, the United States could threaten to inflict massive damage on North Vietnam if it did not halt its support for the NLF. In other words, Johnson's air campaign had a political, rather than a military, objective. He and Robert McNamara strictly controlled the selection of targets to avoid unnecessary casualties and from fear that all-out bombing would provoke Chinese intervention.

The Joint Chiefs of Staff were outraged at this political interference, and their arguments continue to have an effect on Vietnam historiography. C. Dale Walton, in his revisionist book *The Myth of the Inevitable US Defeat in Vietnam* (2002), argues that the war could have been won if Johnson had listened to the advice of the Joint Chiefs. He agrees with Rostow's view that North Vietnam did have important military assets, but blames gradualism for not bombing them, or not bombing them soon enough. In contrast to the gradualist strategy of Rolling Thunder, modern American wars have begun with 'shock-and-awe' tactics, an aerial blitzkrieg to degrade the enemy's command and control centres and destroy its infrastructure at the very beginning of the conflict. So it might be true that America was a chained eagle, at least where bombing was concerned.

What was the purpose of strategic bombing, and why did it not work? Rolling Thunder had four main objectives:

1   To persuade North Vietnam to give up the war and negotiate a peace settlement. But as Kennedy had suspected, North Vietnam had little industry to destroy, getting its weapons from China and the Soviet Union.

2   To cut the Ho Chi Minh Trail, down which supplies and reinforcements were sent into South Vietnam through Laos and Cambodia. This **interdiction** was ineffective; it did not stop supplies from getting through.

Interdiction
Cutting the supply routes through Laos and Cambodia down through which NVA soldiers and supplies for the Viet Cong were sent into South Vietnam.

3   To cut off the supply routes from China and the Soviet Union that came across bridges from China and through the North Vietnamese port of Haiphong. But the Americans did not enjoy total air supremacy over North Vietnam, which deployed MiG fighters and SAM missiles to defend its air space. These increased the risk to American pilots and threw some bombing missions off their targets. The Americans had not yet perfected the laser-guided bombs that struck with such accuracy in the Gulf War of 1991.

4   To undermine civilian support for the war in North Vietnam. But the more the Americans targeted civilians, the louder became the antiwar protests in the United States, encouraging the North to fight on.

In the final months of his presidency, as Johnson tried to negotiate a peace settlement, he tried variously intensifying the bombing and halting it to induce North Vietnam to come to terms. Neither strategy worked.

In the 1970s President Nixon returned to the strategic bombing of North Vietnam with two bombing campaigns, codenamed Linebacker 1 and Linebacker 2. As more and more American troops were withdrawn from Vietnam, Nixon intensified the bombing of major cities like Hanoi and Haiphong to raise morale in South Vietnam and support his policy of Vietnamisation. To achieve this he unleashed 212 B-52 bombers on North Vietnam, half of **SAC**'s strategic bomber force. Despite this intensity the bombing of North Vietnam failed to win the war, though it may have helped to cover the American withdrawal.

SAC
Strategic Air Command, the US Air Force reserve of B-52 bombers designed to strike the Soviet Union with nuclear weapons.

Military strategy before 1968: Attrition

Mention the Vietnam War to most people, and the first thing they will think of is helicopters – especially Hueys, the 'slicks' and 'gunships' that carried soldiers into battle and supported them with airborne weaponry. In 1965 the 1st Battalion, 7th Cavalry Regiment fought the Battle of the Ia Drang Valley, the first major battle between the NVA and the US Army. The American forces were flown by helicopter into a clearing called LZ X-Ray in the Ia Drang Valley, close to a mountain on the Cambodian border where US intelligence reported a build-up of North Vietnamese soldiers. The Army wanted to test its new 'air mobile' tactics against the NVA – it was not disappointed. The NVA commander, too, was eager to test his new enemy. The two armies were soon locked in a life-or-death struggle around the perimeter of LZ X-Ray. The Americans won the battle – they survived the NVA onslaught, killed lots of communists and held LZ X-Ray when the fighting was over.

We Were Soldiers is a film starring Mel Gibson in the role of Lt Col Harold Moore, who commanded the American forces at the Battle of the Ia Drang Valley.

△ American forces often used helicopters to carry soldiers into battle.

The Battle of the Ia Drang Valley played a vital part in establishing the American military strategy between 1965 and 1968. General William Westmoreland, the US commander in Vietnam until 1968, drew conclusions from this battle. Noting that Lt Col Harold Moore's forces killed twelve NVA for every American soldier who died, he calculated that the war could be won by attrition. American firepower – including artillery, fixed-wing aircraft and helicopters – acted as a force multiplier that enabled small American units to fight much larger enemy forces successfully. In the end the communists would give up because their losses would simply be too great.

Westmoreland estimated that it would take about three to four years to defeat the communists. Starting in 1965, the USA would be close to victory in time for the 1968 presidential election. Focused on a daily body count, officers had to prove how many enemy soldiers they had killed. On the basis of these reports, American newspapers produced weekly casualty statistics that appeared to show that America was, indeed, winning the war.

The US Army never seriously tried to hold territory, beyond securing Saigon and the other major cities. If attrition was the strategy, it did not need to – air mobile troops would zoom around South Vietnam, smashing communist forces until their leaders admitted defeat. Time and time again the Americans won a major battle, only to vacate the battlefield and surrender it to their enemies. The strategy made sense if you believed attrition could work, but what if it did not?

The turning point was the Tet Offensive. Throughout 1967 the Viet Cong were building up their forces, preparing for an all-out attack timed to coincide with celebrations for the Chinese New Year. Meanwhile the NVA had the US Marines at Khe Sanh surrounded, threatening to overrun the American base near the DMZ. On 30 January 1968, 84,000 NLF forces attacked every major city, town and American base in South Vietnam, even capturing the American Embassy in Saigon. NVA forces captured the city of Hue and its citadel, which were retaken by the US Marines after fierce fighting.

To learn more about the battle for Hue, watch the BBC programme by Peter and Dan Snow, *20th-Century Battlefields: 1968 Vietnam*.

Eventually the Viet Cong were repulsed and suffered great losses, but the Tet Offensive had enormous consequences. From a purely military point of view it was a great American victory, killing some 40,000 communist troops. Westmoreland was confident that he could finish the job, and asked President Johnson for a further 206,000 troops. But the Tet Offensive shocked the American public, which had no idea that the communists were so strong. The request for additional forces stunned Johnson, precipitating a crisis in the White House that led to McNamara's resignation and Johnson's decision not to run for president in 1968. And in July 1968 General Westmoreland was relieved of his command.

Ever since his replacement, Westmoreland's reputation has been fought over by soldiers and politicians, veterans and armchair strategists, orthodox and revisionist historians. The orthodox view has tended to dominate the argument. David Halberstam, author of *The Best and Brightest* (1972), believed that Westmoreland was too conventional a strategist for a guerrilla war like Vietnam. His strategy of attrition was built on American firepower; consequently he had little interest in counter-insurgency. But the American public wanted results more tangible than body counts. Crucially, he failed to appreciate that a policy of attrition implied a level of US casualties that was not acceptable to the American public. In 1969 *Life* magazine published a large fold-out section – 'One Week's Toll' – containing photographs of all 242 American soldiers killed in one seven-day period. It brought home to the public the fact that a kill ratio of 12:1 was an unacceptable way of looking at the war.

In his memoirs, *A Soldier Reports* (1980), Westmoreland mounted a robust defence of his reputation. His main point was that President Johnson and his aides had given the Army an impossible task: the rules of engagement prevented US forces from crossing into Cambodia or Laos in hot pursuit of the enemy, and an invasion of North Vietnam was ruled out from the start. Communist forces could therefore escape across the borders to a safe haven. Westmoreland also argued that the American public simply did not understand that war involved the use of extreme force. Other military figures rallied to Westmoreland's cause, including Lt Col Moore, who accused Johnson of fighting the war 'on the cheap', refusing to extend enlistments of US soldiers and filling the Army with cannon fodder drawn from conscription.

Revisionist historians have also defended Westmoreland, seeing him as a scapegoat for a failed political policy. Their arguments have focused on the General's supposed failure to appreciate the importance of counter-insurgency and pacification of the countryside. According to historians like Jonathan Caverley and John Carland, this aspect of Westmoreland's reputation has been over-emphasised or misunderstood.

You can see the *Life* magazine photographs 'One Week's Toll' at: http://life.time.com/ history/faces-of-the-american-dead-in-vietnam-one-weeks-toll.

Military strategy after 1968: The 'One War' strategy

By 1969 America had a new president, Richard Nixon, and a new commander in Vietnam, General Creighton Abrams. Abrams introduced a new approach called the 'One War' strategy. To understand it, we need to know a little about the context in which it appeared. We will look at this in more detail in Chapter 5.

President Nixon realised from the start that the Vietnam War was unwinnable, and that America had to find an exit strategy that would enable it to get out of the war without appearing to lose it – what he later called 'peace with honour'. To achieve this, America would have to fight even more aggressively. Many of the constraints that had limited Johnson's options were removed. For example, in 1969 he authorised the secret bombing of Cambodia without the approval of Congress, and in 1970 he allowed the US Army to invade Cambodia, briefly, in pursuit of enemy forces. The bombing of North Vietnam intensified to make up for troop withdrawals in the South. These changes pleased the US military and outraged the American peace movement. This was shown by the Battle of Hamburger Hill in 1969, when US forces stormed a hill in the A Shau Valley, losing 56 dead to kill 700 enemy soldiers, provoking widespread protest in the United States. To please the public he began the process of 'Vietnamisation', a slow, gradual withdrawal of American forces while handing the war over to the ARVN. Simultaneously, a new diplomatic offensive – 'détente' – aimed at driving a wedge between China and the Soviet Union, with a view to ending their support for North Vietnam.

In this context, Abrams' task was to improve the military situation as far as possible in order to strengthen America's hand at the negotiating table. The 'One War' strategy placed greater emphasis on counter-insurgency to pacify the countryside by depriving the Viet Cong of civilian support. Working more closely with the South Vietnamese Army, the Americans tried to follow up their military operations by training and equipping self-defence forces in Vietnamese villages, while the Civilian Operations and Revolutionary Development Support (CORDS) extended the hearts and minds campaign by working towards village economic development. Targeting the Viet Cong infrastructure at village level, the so-called Phoenix programme led to the capture of 34,000 Viet Cong supporters and the assassination of a number of high-level communist cadres. Abrams replaced Westmoreland's strategy of attrition, which used large-scale, multi-battalion search-and-destroy missions, with patrols by smaller units and ambushes aimed at providing villages with greater security. A new emphasis was placed on the taking and holding of territory, gradually extending pacified villages to link up with each other and deprive the enemy of taxes, rice and other essentials. Furthermore, greater cooperation was encouraged between the US Army and the US Marines, who had spearheaded the idea of embedding small squads of Marines with local defence forces. These were important changes in the way the Americans fought, but they came too late to prevent the collapse of South Vietnam in 1975. As we shall see, however, they did contribute to America's exit strategy.

The 'One War' strategy has provoked considerable debate among historians. The orthodox view is that it came too late to salvage a failing war: public support for the war in the USA was crumbling and time was running out for the Americans. At the same time, morale in the US Army was collapsing. It is also argued that General Abrams' strategy was not really that different from Westmoreland's. Set against this are various revisionist arguments claiming that America had virtually won the war by 1973, only to have defeat snatched from the jaws of victory in the two years after the Americans pulled out. This 'lost victory' thesis can be traced back to William Colby, head of the CORDS programme from 1968, who argued that the many initiatives dating from around 1968 had achieved security for most South Vietnamese villages by 1970. The lost victory thesis has many problems, but it reflects the refusal of many Americans to accept that their armed forces were defeated in the Vietnam War.

▇ Now we need to put the finishing touches to our folder on the USA. How did the American war effort contribute to America's defeat in Vietnam? In your notes you should include some judgements on the following points:

- The failure of the hearts and minds programme to win widespread support for the South Vietnamese Government.
- America's strategic bombing of North Vietnam. Should the president have given the US military free choice of its targets? And should the bombing campaign have been massive from the start, or was Johnson right to adopt Rostow's gradualist approach?

- The failure of General Westmoreland's strategy of attrition and the rules of engagement set by President Johnson – for example, the decision not to invade North Vietnam and the decision not to allow the US Army to pursue communist forces into Cambodia or Laos.

- The 'One War' strategy. Was this a case of 'too little, too late'?

Concluding your enquiry

The idea that America defeated itself in Vietnam is not as stupid as it sounds. We have now examined the three nations most closely involved in the conflict, and we have seen that the American war effort, in particular, is highly controversial. There is not a single aspect of the war that American historians have not argued about.

You should now have collected ideas and information in each of the three folders with which we opened the enquiry. Now you need to make up your mind about the conclusions you have reached:

- **South Vietnam.** Was America shackled to a corpse? Was South Vietnam ever a country that was likely to be able to stand up to North Vietnam and the NLF? In simple terms, did America back a loser?

- **North Vietnam.** Could the Americans have defeated the communists? Or did the strategy and tactics the communists used make an American victory impossible?

- **The USA.** Was America a chained eagle? Did the politicians prevent the military from winning the war? Or do you think that this is the military's way of shifting the blame for their own mistakes?

Why did the USA lose the Vietnam War? This is the question with which we began this chapter. Did America 'blow it'? Reviewing all the evidence, if America had used different strategies, do you think it could have won the war? If the answer is 'yes', then it is reasonable to conclude that America did defeat itself by choosing the wrong strategies.

We need to bear in mind the fact that the American strategy was clearly failing up until 1968. This meant that the first three years of the war were wasted. It also meant that the American public had virtually given up on the war by the time the 'One War' strategy was used.

It is understandable that the US military tried to shift the blame for America's defeat from their own shoulders onto those of America's political leaders. In 200 years of warfare this was the first war America had ever lost. It was a new type of war, a war of limited objectives that had to be fought with restraint. But this should not blind us to the responsibility the US military itself bears for the defeat. It was the Army that chose to pursue a strategy of attrition. Fresh from its victory in the Second World War, the military was over-confident in its use of firepower. The politicians who made these decisions are long gone, but the military has an ongoing interest in defending its reputation. This being so, we must be wary of the easy option of condemning those who can no longer defend themselves.

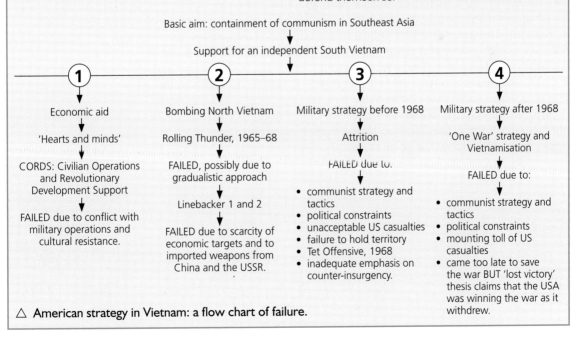

△ **American strategy in Vietnam: a flow chart of failure.**

Counterfactual history and the Vietnam War

Imagine the following scenario. In 1965, after his landslide electoral victory, President Johnson goes to Congress and asks for a declaration of war against North Vietnam. Congress agrees, and with America now formally at war, Johnson mobilises the National Guard, calls up all the reservists, extends the draft, censors the press and redeploys troops from West Germany to Southeast Asia. Giving in to the Pentagon, he immediately begins a full-scale bombing campaign of North Vietnam. The US Army goes into South Vietnam with 800,000 men. American troops invade Laos to cut the Ho Chi Minh Trail, and the military is given complete freedom to pursue communist forces across the border into Cambodia. With the US Navy threatening the North Vietnamese coast, the US Army invades North Vietnam. If China threatens to intervene, America threatens Beijing with nuclear weapons. This, according to a generalised revisionist thesis, is what the United States should have done. What might have happened if it did?

Hypothetical questions like these are called 'counterfactual history', because they run counter to the known facts. For many years professional historians rejected this approach; they argued that it drew people away from the actual evidence, away from the *history*. E.P. Thompson, author of *The Making of the English Working Class* (1963), referred to counterfactual history as 'unhistorical shit'. In recent years counterfactual history has found more favour with historians. In 1997 Niall Ferguson edited *Virtual History: Alternatives and Counterfactuals* in which several distinguished historians used it as an analytical tool. Ferguson defended the practice with these words: 'Because decisions about the future are – usually – based on weighing up the potential consequences of alternative courses of action, it makes sense to compare the actual outcomes of what we did in the past with the conceivable outcomes of what we might have done.'

What were 'the conceivable outcomes of what we might have done' in Vietnam? The generalised revisionist thesis outlined above argues that America would have won the war. Assuming that China did not intervene, overwhelming force would have quickly overpowered the NVA and the NLF. If China did intervene, given the fact that it had no nuclear weapons in the 1960s, it would surely have backed down in the face of certain destruction.

We then have to ask ourselves a question that is not hypothetical, but factual. We know that Johnson took a more belligerent stance than Kennedy, so why did he not go all the way?

And finally … what do I think?

What follows is a purely personal answer to this question. In my own opinion, each of the courses of action recommended by this generalised revisionist view has compelling objections, which I will outline briefly:

- **Declaring war on North Vietnam.** The USA has not declared war on any country since 1942, yet it has fought wars in Korea, Vietnam, Iraq (twice) and Afghanistan and taken military action in Grenada, Panama, Lebanon and Libya. Congress would be unlikely to declare war on any country that had not actually attacked the United States – which North Vietnam had not done, despite the Gulf of Tonkin incident and the attack on the American air base at Pleiku in 1965.

- **Mobilising the USA for war.** The cost of a full-scale mobilisation would have destroyed the Great Society programme of domestic reforms, which was Johnson's most important domestic agenda.

- **Unrestricted bombing of North Vietnam.** Johnson rejected this because he believed such bombing was unreasonable and unnecessary. After the Cuban Missile Crisis he was wary of giving the military control over an essentially political objective. I believe that Kennedy was right: the prospect of the United States bombing North Vietnam mercilessly from the start would have caused international outrage.

- **Sending 800,000 men to South Vietnam.** To raise an army of 800,000 men would have seriously depleted the US Army in West Germany, exposing NATO to greater danger of a Soviet attack in Europe.

- **Invading Laos and Cambodia.** The Vietnam War was fought to prevent the 'domino theory' spreading communism throughout Southeast Asia. Invading these countries would have strengthened communist movements there – exactly what happened when Nixon authorised limited invasions.

- **Invading North Vietnam.** This would surely have provoked Chinese intervention in the war. In Korea the Chinese had fought the Americans to a standstill. Why would Vietnam be any different?

- **Threatening China with nuclear weapons.** In 1962 the USA narrowly avoided a nuclear war with the Soviet Union during the Cuban Missile Crisis. Johnson was genuinely frightened by this crisis and acutely aware of the danger of nuclear confrontation – if not with China then with China's ally, the Soviet Union.

It is hard to avoid the conclusion that President Johnson was right not to follow such an extreme course. That then begs the question: should he have sent US soldiers to fight in Vietnam in the first place? We will examine that issue at the end of Chapter 4 in another counterfactual Insight (pages 77–78).

Reading the Vietnam War

The best way to develop your interest in the Vietnam War is to read stories about it written by people who were there. The generation of Americans that fought in Vietnam was probably the best-educated, most literate generation in American history. Many former soldiers have published memoirs and novels based on their experiences. Once you start, you will not be able to stop. So get reading!

'We'll see who's chickenshit,' China said. He pulled the pin of the grenade and everything seemed to go in slow motion for him … He was only dimly aware of people shouting, running, scrambling for the door of the tent. "He's f***** crazy, man! A f***** frag goin' off! Jesus Christ!' China, his tongue on his lips, concentrating on the count, tossed the grenade back to Henry and watched the spoon fly off toward the side of the tent.

Karl Marlantes, *Matterhorn* (2010)

You can say what you want about the M-16 rifle. It does jam a lot in fire fights, but it can also put out some heat in a hurry. If you want to light some guy up, there is no better way than with an M-16. It fires so quickly, the guy is dead before he hits the ground. AK-47s (Charlie's rifle) and our M-60 machine guns knock guys around and tear them up. M-16s just do 'em. Instant Christmas tree.

Ernest Spencer, *Welcome to Vietnam, Macho Man* (1987)

After enough time passed and memory receded and settled, the name itself became a prayer, coded like all prayer to go past the extremes of petition and gratitude: Vietnam Vietnam Vietnam, say again, until the word lost all its old loads of pain, pleasure, horror, guilt, nostalgia. Then and there, everyone was just trying to get through it, existential crunch, no atheists in foxholes like you wouldn't believe. Even bitter refracted faith was better than none at all, like the black Marine I'd heard about during heavy shelling at Con Thien who said, 'Don't worry, baby, God'll think of something.'

Michael Herr, *Dispatches* (1977)

From a kilometre away, the sonic roar of the B-52 explosions tore eardrums, leaving many of the jungle dwellers permanently deaf. From a kilometre, the shock waves knocked their victims senseless … The first few times I experienced a B-52 attack it seemed, as I strained to press myself into the bunker floor, that I had been caught in the Apocalypse. The terror was complete. One lost control of bodily functions as the mind screamed incomprehensible orders to get out.

Truong Nhu Tang, *A Vietcong Memoir* (1985)

Then it happened. The platoon exploded. It was a collective emotional detonation of men who had been pushed to the extremity of endurance. I lost control of them and even of myself. Desperate to get to the hill, we rampaged through the rest of the village, whooping like savages, torching thatch huts, tossing grenades into the cement houses we could not burn. In our frenzy, we crashed through the hedgerows without feeling the stabs of the thorns. We did not feel anything. We were past feeling for ourselves, let alone for others. We shut our ears to the cries and pleas of the villagers. One elderly man ran up to me, and, grabbing me by the front of my shirt, asked, 'Tai Sao? Tai Sao?' Why? Why?
'Get out of my goddamned way,' I said, pulling his hands off. I took hold of his shirt and flung him down hard, feeling as if I were watching myself in a movie. The man lay where he fell, crying, 'Tai Sao? Tai Sao?'

Philip Caputo, *A Rumour of War* (1977)

Little did Willoughby, Jim Flynn, or any of the others know that this moment in history was changing forever the way Americans would view their government leaders. In years to come, cynicism and doubt would creep into people's minds whenever American forces were ordered to take the battlefield during foreign wars, ethnic clashes, and police actions that would put American kids unnecessarily at risk.

John Culbertson, *13 Cent Killers* (2003)

'What do people want when they send me to fight out there?' he would ask, growling. 'To search out and destroy the enemy.' 'Yeah, yeah, I know that. But what do they want when the enemy is ten years old and has big tits – women and children, you know. What then? What if *they're* the enemy?' 'Well, you kill them or capture them. But you only do that when they're engaged in combat, sir. It's a civil war, in part, and even if some of them come down from North Vietnam, they look like the South Vietnamese. So you've got to assume –' 'Assume, bullshit! When you go into My Lai you assume the *worst*.'

Tim O'Brien, *If I Die in a Combat Zone* (1973)

I sucked in all of the air in that tunnel. My hand flew to my throat. My heart nearly jumped out of my chest. Staring back at me were four North Vietnamese Army regulars in full uniform, with AK-47 rifles, grenades, and hand-held rocket launchers! I froze. I did not dare to breathe. I looked again, hoping to God the marijuana was playing tricks on my head. Sure as shit, they were there; and they looked as surprised and panicky as I felt. One of them, with a whole assortment of glittery brass oak leaf clusters on his collar, grinned broadly and put his index finger to his lips in the universal sign for quiet. Another, also breaking into a broad grin, held out a bottle of Bam-Be-Bam [beer].

John Ketwig, *...and a hard rain fell* (2002)

We picked up the troopers at the Tea Plantation, eight to each Huey. It was easy to tell where we were going. Although we were still fifteen miles away, the smoke was clearly visible from all the artillery, B-52 bombers, and gunship support concentrated around the LZ to keep the grunts from being overrun. As we cruised over the jungles and fields of elephant grass, I had the feeling this was a movie scene: the gentle rise and fall of the Hueys as we cruised, the perspective created by looking along the formation of ships to the smoke on the horizon, the quiet. None of the crews talked on the radios. We all listened to the urgent voices in the static as they called in air strikes and artillery on their own perimeters, then yelled that the rounds were hitting in their positions.

Robert Mason, *Chickenhawk* (1983)

Julie talks of those days as a time of fear, a time when the mere sight of a Yellow Cab cruising through the neighbourhood struck panic in the hearts of the wives and children of soldiers serving in Vietnam. As the taxicabs and telegrams spread misery and grief, Julie followed them to the trailer courts and thin-walled apartment complexes and boxy bungalows, doing her best to comfort those whose lives had been destroyed.

Lt Gen Harold Moore and Joseph Galloway, *We Were Soldiers Once ... and Young* (1992)

3 What impact did the Vietnam War have on America?

▷ The actress Jane Fonda sitting on a North Vietnamese anti-aircraft gun in 1972.

Guernica

A town in Spain that was bombed by Hitler's air force in 1938. It was the first time in history that a civilian population was bombed intensively, an event immortalised in a painting by Picasso.

In England Jane Fonda is known as a famous actress and author of *Jane Fonda's Workout Book*. Her films – *Barbarella*, *Klute*, *Monster-in-Law* – made her a household name. Her face peers out from a thousand L'Oreal adverts as the face that never ages. In America, though, she is also known as 'Hanoi Jane'. In 1972 Jane Fonda visited North Vietnam as an antiwar protest against the American Government. Dozens of American bombers were raging across the skies of North Vietnam, dropping thousands of tonnes of bombs on Hanoi and other cities. The sight of the world's most powerful nation relentlessly bombing a Third World country reminded Fonda and many other people of the Nazi bombing of **Guernica** in the Spanish Civil War, just as President Kennedy feared it would (see page 32).

Fonda was pictured sitting on a North Vietnamese anti-aircraft gun, laughing and clapping her hands in apparent delight, peering through the gun sight of a weapon that was used to shoot down American planes. She later claimed that the photos were misleading, and apologised to American veterans and former prisoners of war for the distress caused. But the images did enormous damage to her reputation in America, where some people still refer to her as the 'Traitor Bitch'. The passions unleashed by

42

Fonda's visit to North Vietnam are symbolic of the deep divisions caused in America by the Vietnam War.

America went through extraordinary changes in the ten years from 1965 to 1975. The most visible change was in the culture of young people – their music, behaviour, values and attitudes towards authority. Student protests swept the campuses of American universities, leading to violence and even death. America's social cohesion appeared to fall apart in the riots of the 'long hot summers', the assassinations of American leaders and the violence of political discourse. In 1965 most Americans still believed that politicians were essentially decent, honest people; by 1975 this trust had been largely replaced by cynicism, aided by the **Watergate Affair** in the early 1970s. During these years a fundamental shift towards right-wing politics was taking place, especially in the South. In the quest for civil rights Black Power emerged to defy and challenge the non-violent protests of Martin Luther King and his followers. In this decade, too, the American economy ran into problems: manufacturing industry felt the impact of the post-war economic recovery of West Germany and Japan, and of the rising cost of oil. The USA passed from having a national fiscal surplus to a permanent national debt, as government spending outpaced revenue. A crime wave seemed to threaten the security of ordinary people, whose fears were fuelled by incidents like the **Manson murders**.

Watergate Affair
The political scandal that led to the resignation of President Richard Nixon in 1974.

Manson murders
The notorious killing in Los Angeles of the actress Sharon Tate and some of her friends by a drug-crazed gang led by Charles Manson.

■ Enquiry Focus: What impact did the Vietnam War have on America?

It just so happens that the period 1965 to 1975 was the decade of the Vietnam War. The question arises, then, how far the war was responsible for these changes. This is a big question. You are not trying to explain some historical EVENT like a revolution or a war by looking at the factors that caused it. Rather, you are trying to weigh up the IMPACT of the event itself – a more difficult problem. It is an important question, one that divides historians today just as it divided the people who lived through these events. Was late 1960s America simply the CONTEXT in which the Vietnam War was fought, or did the war SHAPE THE CONTEXT – and if so, to what extent?

This chapter is divided into sections exploring the impact of the war on four aspects of American society – the student movement, the economy, politics and the civil rights movement. For each section you need to collect material to help you reach conclusions about how far the Vietnam War affected the changes that were taking place. As you work through each section, make notes to help you answer the following questions:

- What changes were happening during this period?
- How did the Vietnam War affect these changes?
- What other influences affected these changes?

At the end of the chapter you will complete a diagram to summarise the relative impact of the Vietnam War on these four aspects of recent American history. To do this effectively, you need to collect material about each aspect under the three headings above. You will then write an essay about the impact the Vietnam War had on America during the late 1960s and early 1970s.

The student movement

When we were kids the United States was the wealthiest and strongest country in the world: the only one with the atom bomb, the least scarred by modern war, an initiator of the United Nations that we thought would distribute Western influence throughout the world. Freedom and equality for each individual, government of, by, and for the people – these American values we found good. As we grew, however, our comfort was penetrated by events too troubling to dismiss.

First, the fact of human degradation, symbolised by the Southern struggle against racial bigotry, compelled most of us from silence to activism. Second, the enclosing fact of the Cold War, symbolised by the presence of the Bomb, brought awareness that we ourselves, and our friends, and millions of abstract 'others', might die at any time.

We also began to see complicated and disturbing paradoxes in our surrounding America. The declaration 'all men are created equal...' rang hollow before the facts of Negro life in the South and the big cities of the North. The proclaimed peaceful intentions of the United States contradicted its economic and military investments in the Cold War status quo. While two-thirds of mankind suffers hunger, our own upper classes revel amid superfluous abundance, and uncontrolled exploitation is sapping the Earth's physical resources.

This is an extract from the Port Huron Statement, issued by Students for a Democratic Society (SDS) in 1962. It tells us something about the things that students found disturbing as they grew up. It also tells us that the student movement began before American combat troops were sent to the Vietnam War.

Folk protest songs by musicians such as Bob Dylan, Joan Baez, Peter, Paul and Mary, and Tom Paxton were already very popular by 1963. Many students were politicised by events in the 1950s, especially the campaign for black civil rights. The 1950s also saw the birth of rock 'n' roll, which the older generation thought was outrageous, and the rise of Beatnik poets such as Allen Ginsberg, protesting against perceived injustices. At this stage the student movement was inspired by non-violent civil rights protests. There was naïve optimism that the world could be changed for the better, if only people made the right choices.

Student deferment

High-school graduates who were eligible for the draft could apply to 'defer' or put off their military service until after university, in the hope that by then the war would be over.

Antiwar protests

The war in Vietnam galvanised the student movement and turned many student protests into violent confrontations with the police. Students felt it was their civic duty to question the war. There was a growing suspicion that the US Government had lied to the public. Some of America's methods aroused indignation, especially the bombing of North Vietnam and the use of napalm.

Alongside these moral and intellectual objections, there was the threat of being drafted. Most of the American soldiers serving in Vietnam were draftees. Every teenage American boy growing up in the late 1960s and early 1970s faced the threat of being drafted and sent to Vietnam. Many students burned their draft cards in protest, or fled to Canada to escape conscription. The draft system itself deepened American social divisions. Realistically, only white middle-class high-school graduates could win places at colleges and universities and gain **student deferments**. This ensured that it was mostly working-class men who fought the war, with a disproportionately high number of blacks, a fact that fuelled the Black Power movement.

Timeline of American history, 1962–75

1962	Cuban Missile Crisis – world comes to the brink of nuclear war
	Students for a Democratic Society (SDS) publish their Port Huron Statement
1963	Civil rights – police brutality against black demonstrators in Birmingham, Alabama
	Civil rights – Martin Luther King's 'Dream' speech at the March for Jobs and Freedom in Washington DC
	President Kennedy assassinated – Lyndon Johnson takes over as president
1964	President Johnson re-elected in a landslide victory
	Johnson announces the Great Society programme
	Gulf of Tonkin incident
	Congress passes the Civil Rights Act
1965	President Johnson commits US combat forces to the Vietnam War
	Congress passes the Voting Rights Act
	'Teach-in' movement begins in American universities
1966	SDS begins resistance against the draft
1967	Martin Luther King denounces the Vietnam War
	Antiwar demonstration, University of Wisconsin
	Vietnam Veterans Against the War founded
	Large antiwar demonstration outside the Pentagon
1968	President Johnson announces he will not run for a second term
	Martin Luther King assassinated – widespread city race riots
	Robert Kennedy assassinated
	Riots in Chicago at the Democratic Party's national convention to select a presidential candidate
	Richard Nixon elected president
1969	Weathermen form splinter group from SDS and begin bombing campaign against US government buildings
	Apollo 11 lands on the moon
	250,000 march against the war in Washington DC
1970	Four students shot dead during antiwar demonstration at Kent State University, Ohio
	President Nixon makes impromptu visit to meet protestors at the Lincoln Memorial
1971	Half a million people take part in an antiwar protest march in Washington DC
	New York Times publishes the Pentagon Papers
1972	Watergate break-in
	George McGovern runs for president on an antiwar ticket
	Nixon re-elected president
1973	Last US troops leave Vietnam
1974	President Nixon resigns because of the Watergate Affair
1975	South Vietnam defeated

The battle for history

The riot at the University of Wisconsin illustrates the way that historical debates can get started. You would think it would be easy to ascertain the facts of what happened: there were hundreds of witnesses, and the incident was filmed by television news. But the events of that day are hotly disputed.

In October 1967 a student antiwar demonstration at the University of Wisconsin spiralled out of control. The Dow Chemical Company, which manufactured napalm, was sending its people to the university campus to recruit graduates. Some of the students organised a sit-in protest; the university authorities called the police. Ordered to clear the building, the police attacked the students, cracking heads and kneecaps with their truncheons. This 'police brutality' drew hundreds more students into the protest, many of them shouting 'Sieg heil!' and throwing back the tear gas canisters now being fired into the demonstration. It was a turning point.

From now on student protests across the country regularly turned into violent confrontations. The antiwar movement spread beyond the campuses, and branches of it became violent. In 1969 a group called the Weathermen split from SDS and conducted a bombing campaign against government buildings. The Vietnam War split the nation into opponents and supporters, creating deep social divisions.

The context in which this happened was explosive, because in the 1960s a counter-cultural revolution was taking place in the United States, one that was bitterly resisted by the forces of tradition, religion and patriotism. This counter-culture consisted of two distinct but interacting strands. Firstly, from the protest movements of the early 1960s there emerged a left-wing neo-socialist moral crusade that attacked the Establishment and its injustices. Inspired by the civil rights movement, it originally focused on perceived miscarriages of justice like Sacco and Vanzetti or Rubin 'Hurricane' Carter, building on the anticapitalist traditions of singers like Woody Guthrie and books like *The Grapes of Wrath*. It also drew support from church-oriented peace movements like the Quakers, and from older pacifist or antinuclear protest groups. After 1965 the Vietnam War became its main target, an expression of 'the System' that subjugated civil liberties and social justice to the needs of American capitalism.

But what really gave the Vietnam era its distinctive feel was the emergence of a second counter-cultural movement based around hallucinatory drugs like LSD and marijuana, rock music (as distinct from rock 'n' roll), Eastern mysticism, hippie communes and *The Thoughts of Chairman Mao*, all popular because they held out the prospect of instantaneous revolution. By 1965 this New Left student movement was established as the leader of antiwar protests. For a substantial proportion of American youth, the world was perceived through a miasma of dope, acid and rock lyrics. At the extreme end of the scale, the counter-cultural revolution encouraged nihilistic suicide, murderous groups like the Manson Family, anarchists and violent terrorists like the Weathermen, who organised a 'Days of Rage' bombing campaign in 1969.

The US Government, and especially President Nixon, saw the counter-culture as a direct threat to American national security. Nixon even employed Elvis Presley as a special agent to combat alien influences in popular music, and waged war on John Lennon by denying him a visa to live in the United States. During many demonstrations – the University of Wisconsin in 1967, the Democratic National Convention in Chicago in 1968, Kent State University in Ohio in 1970 – the police reacted to antiwar protests with disproportionate violence.

At the University of Wisconsin the students blamed the police for attacking a peaceful sit-in demonstration. Film of the incident appears to confirm that the police attacked the students and used excessive violence. The police told a different story. They said the demonstration was organised by outside agitators spoiling for a fight. They were ordered to clear the building. They saw the students as privileged rich kids and intellectuals who could avoid the draft, unlike the police themselves who came from mostly working-class districts.

Mark Greenside, one of the students, commented on how the riot was reported, and how these reports fuelled the student movement itself:

> In the days after Dow the newspapers came out with stories that essentially blamed the students for what happened and blamed us for provoking it and causing it and for attacking the police and making them have to defend themselves against us, and it just added to the credibility gap that we already felt with all the institutions of authority.

To gain an insight into the role of veterans in the antiwar movement, watch the Oliver Stone film *Born on the Fourth of July*, based on the story of Ron Kovic, a member of Vietnam Veterans Against the War.

During the 1970s the student movement largely gave way to Vietnam Veterans Against the War, founded in 1967. Men who had actually fought in Vietnam had greater public credibility than students, who many people regarded as draft-dodgers and 'lefties'. Many veterans returned their medals in protest, and their opposition to the war was more difficult for the authorities to dismiss.

Forty-three years later, the author looks back on the draft

Getting drafted and sent to Vietnam was a national lottery, with Death on the winning ticket. Each year we crowded around a transistor radio and listened while the president, or the leader of the Senate, or the leader of the Senate's wife, or the leader of the Senate's wife's first cousin's best friend, drew 365 plastic pellets out of a barrel. Each pellet contained a calendar date for the coming year. If you were male and your number came up, and you could not get a student deferment or concoct some outrageous medical problem, you might as well pack your bags. As the war drew closer, we planned our escape routes. I was going to join the Coast Guard and spend my service years rescuing little kids blown out to sea on inflatable mattresses. Randy was going to join the Air Force and bomb the shit out of the bastards from 40,000 feet. Steve would apply for a student deferment. Mike was pinning his hopes on his fallen arches. Charlie would get out of it because he was too simple to be trusted with a rifle.

△ The author, aged sixteen in 1972: his long hair and combat jacket expressed the ambiguity he felt about the war in Vietnam.

Economic changes

During the 1964 election Johnson promised to build a 'Great Society' in America. This society would bring an end to poverty and racial injustice. It would be a land of educational opportunity for all children, a place where American liberty and productivity could enrich the lives of all citizens. The Great Society would create a greater sense of community and beauty, a destiny where 'the meaning of our lives matches the marvellous products of our labour'. And it would be expensive.

Johnson's vision of America's future was rooted in his Democratic Party career. As a young man in the 1930s he worked for President Roosevelt's New Deal. He served President Truman's Fair Deal in the 1940s and President Kennedy's New Frontier. The Great Society, he hoped, would be the next great phase of America's development, one where the 'pursuit of happiness' could be made a tangible objective.

The Train Robbery

△ 'The Train Robbery': a cartoon from *Punch* magazine.

This cartoon expresses a commonly held belief that the Vietnam War destroyed Johnson's Great Society programme. In 1967 Martin Luther King said that the war was doing irreparable harm to Johnson's programmes aimed at poverty, education and housing. Johnson himself said much the same thing: 'I knew from the start that if I left a woman I really loved – the Great Society – in order to fight that bitch of a war in Vietnam then I would lose everything at home. My hopes and dreams.'

Did the Vietnam War destroy the Great Society programme? There is no doubt that some of the money that might have been spent on the 'war on poverty', housing and education was directed instead to pay for the war. However, the achievements of the Johnson presidency were substantial: between 1960 and 1968 Federal aid to the poor rose from $10 billion to $30 billion; 2 million children benefited from the Head Start programme to provide pre-school education for the poor; and Congress passed the vast majority of the president's proposed legislation, including the Civil Rights and Voting Rights Acts. Politics, however, is largely a matter of perception. If you were poor, or black, or unemployed, there is a good chance that you blamed the Vietnam War for the Government's inability to solve your problems. Johnson's tragedy was that the most liberal president of the twentieth century lost the support of his liberal base, and the Vietnam War was the reason. Also, the war undoubtedly monopolised Johnson's energy and time and that of his chief advisors. This is probably what he meant when he said he 'left a woman I really loved'.

We should also place the war into the broader context of global economic changes. Immediately after 1945 the United States enjoyed a period of about 15 years when its main industrial competitors were reeling from the effects of the Second World War. Germany and Japan were in ruins. Britain was financially exhausted, its industry tired and uncompetitive. The Soviet Union and communist China were planned economies that did not participate in the global capitalist system. Consequently, allowing for the rise and fall of the business cycle, America enjoyed a period of rapid economic growth.

During the 1960s and early 1970s this situation was quickly changing. West Germany and Japan became serious international competitors. On the streets of American cities Volkswagen Beetles and Japanese motorbikes challenged the supremacy of American industry. By the 1970s American industrial cities like Detroit, Allentown and Norfolk were struggling against competition from 'Pacific Rim' countries like Japan, Taiwan and South Korea. Then in 1973 the Yom Kippur War in the Middle East sent the international price of oil rocketing, leading to rapid price inflation. Caught unprepared as consumers turned their backs on American gas-guzzlers, the automotive industry went into crisis, which affected the whole economy. By the mid-1970s Americans looked back on the pre-Vietnam era as a kind of economic golden age.

How far was the war responsible for America's relative economic decline? Some economists have said that it helped tip the balance at a time when the economy faced major challenges. Resources that could have been available for consumer production were diverted towards war material. The war was an inflationary pressure that contributed to rising prices. The US Government found it could no longer afford the costs of the welfare state, the Cold War and the Vietnam War, forcing the Federal Reserve to increase the national debt.

On the other hand, it has been argued that the Vietnam War was good for business. Defence contracts to keep the war supplied with helicopters, M-16 rifles, Skyhawk and Phantom jets, napalm and high explosives provided employment and helped American industry adjust to foreign competition. More radical interpretations of the Vietnam War emphasise the economic benefits of the conflict; some even go so far as to suggest that the underlying American motive for involvement was the pressure to protect the expanding markets of the 'Pacific Rim' and open them up to American competition.

A political crisis

On 31 March 1968 President Johnson went on TV to promote peace talks. He announced that the United States was halting the bombing of North Vietnam immediately. At the end of the speech Johnson shocked the nation with a statement that took everyone by surprise:

With America's sons in the fields far away, with America's future under challenge right here at home, with our hopes and the world's hopes for peace in the balance every day, I do not believe that I should devote an hour or a day of my time to any personal partisan causes or to any duties other than the awesome duties of this office – the Presidency of your country. Accordingly, I shall not seek, and I will not accept, the nomination of my party for another term as your President.

For Johnson to do this was extraordinary: he had worked towards the presidency all his adult life, a consummate politician with a special gift for persuading others to do what he wanted. Now it seemed that he was throwing away the ultimate prize, and changing course in the Vietnam War while he did so. Why did Johnson make this dramatic change?

On 27 February a historic meeting had been held in the White House between the president's leading foreign-policy advisors – Robert McNamara, the chief architect of the war and now the outgoing secretary of defence; his successor, Clark Clifford; the national security adviser, Walt Rostow; and others. On 30 January the Tet Offensive had broken the illusion that the war was going well. Public support for the war appeared to be collapsing. Yet the US military believed America had just achieved a huge victory. One more surge, they thought, would bring the war to an end. To achieve this, General Westmoreland and General Wheeler, Chairman of the Joint Chiefs of Staff, asked Johnson to authorise the call-up of a further 206,000 troops. This would bring American forces in Vietnam to nearly 700,000 men.

Johnson was stunned by the request. A conflict that began as a low-level counter-insurgency mission had turned into a huge war. Robert McNamara was leaving office because he now realised that it was a terrible mistake. America, he said, should declare victory and get out. When challenged by Walt Rostow, who wanted to intensify the bombing campaign, McNamara burst into tears. Clark Clifford, the new secretary of defence, asked about the Government's exit strategy and was told that there wasn't one. America was adrift in a sea of blood.

The 1968 election promised to be the most partisan election in modern history. Against a background of riots, civil rights protests, political extremism, assassinations, antiwar protests and the failure of the Great Society, the Democratic Party split into factions. Johnson probably realised that he would lose if he stood for re-election, but it is also true that he and his policies stood in the way of peace. So on 31 March he quit the race for re-election.

The big picture

American politics went through enormous changes in the decade from 1965 to 1975. In the short term these changes were very dramatic. In 1968 the Republican candidate Richard Nixon won the presidential election. During the election campaign Robert Kennedy was assassinated, moments after giving a speech in California attacking the Vietnam War. Coming just four months after the assassination of Martin Luther King, the nation was traumatised by violence. On the streets outside the 1968 Democratic national convention in Chicago a riot broke out when the police tried to break up antiwar demonstrators. It seemed like American society was split down the middle between conservatives and liberals. Four years later, in 1972, the Republican national convention in Miami provoked similar protests and violence. In that year, as Nixon sought re-election, members of Nixon's re-election team conducted an illegal campaign of 'dirty tricks' against the Democrats that became known as the Watergate Affair. This led to Nixon's resignation in 1974.

Against this background, American politics was going through a major realignment of political forces. Ever since the Civil War, the South had been a Democratic Party stronghold, due to its opposition to the abolition of slavery by the Republican President Lincoln. After Kennedy's assassination in 1963, President Johnson persuaded Congress to pass the Civil Rights Act of 1964 as a tribute to the slain president. Johnson used all his political experience to persuade his fellow Southerners to overcome their long-standing opposition to civil rights legislation. It was a major triumph, one that helped to shape America as it is today, but the consequences for the national Democratic Party were disastrous. Across the South, life-long Democrats questioned their allegiance to the Democratic Party. In 1968 this was expressed in support for the independent candidate George Wallace who, as Governor of Alabama, had resisted the integration of the public school system. In the long term many Southerners switched to the Republican Party as the party most in touch with their conservative ideals. In the half-century since 1965 American conservatives have shifted even further to the right. The legacy of the 1960s is that, today, America is more divided politically than at any time since the abolition of slavery.

Between them, the Vietnam War and the Watergate Affair had other serious effects on American politics. In the 1970s Congress passed several Acts to 'rein in' the presidency and reassert congressional supervision of the president's powers:

- **The War Powers Act, 1973.** The president must inform Congress within 48 hours of committing US armed forces to military action. If Congress does not authorise the use of military force, armed conflict must end within 60 days. This resolution encourages American presidents to fight short, decisive wars such as the Gulf War of 1991 – hence the shift from 'gradualist' bombing campaigns to 'shock-and-awe' tactics.
- **The Freedom of Information Act, 1974.** The US Government must make available to the public all information it holds about US citizens.
- **The National Emergencies Act, 1976.** During a declared national emergency, the president has special powers to take decisions. When it was discovered that the presidency had been operating under a continuous open-ended state of emergency since 1950, Congress passed this Act to regulate the declaration of national emergencies.

The psychological impact of Vietnam and Watergate was arguably even more important. By 1975 the American people had become much more cynical about politicians. This was reflected in the aggressiveness of journalism and the willingness to consider personal behaviour, especially sexual impropriety, as a matter of public concern.

The civil rights movement

On 4 April 1967 Martin Luther King made a speech at Riverside Church in New York City. In contrast to his more famous speeches, King read out a carefully worded statement attacking the war in Vietnam. Slowly and methodically he explained how his conscience left him no other choice, attacking the war as an enemy of the poor. Concerning non-violence, he said, 'I knew that I could never again raise my voice against the violence of the oppressed in the ghettos without having first spoken clearly to the greatest purveyor of violence in the world today – my own government.' He tore into the history of American policy in Vietnam, describing as 'strange liberators' the American forces that were laying waste to the country they were trying to save. There was, he said, a very obvious connection between the Vietnam War and the struggle for civil rights in America, and he voiced his concerns about the effect the war was having on American soldiers. 'We are adding cynicism to the process of death,' he said, 'for they must know after a short period there that none of the things we claim to be fighting for are really involved.'

King did not limit his attack to Vietnam. The war was a symptom of a far deeper malady within the American spirit. America, he said, always seemed to be on the wrong side. A worldwide revolution was taking place in which Third World peoples were fighting to overthrow colonialism and redistribute wealth more fairly. America was using Cold War rhetoric to justify its opposition to revolution in order to protect its investments overseas. He called upon America to undergo a radical revolution of values, from a 'thing-oriented' to a 'person-oriented' society. 'When machines and computers, profit motives and property rights are considered more important than people,' he said, 'the giant triplets of racism, materialism and militarism are incapable of being conquered.'

With this speech, King became the most eloquent and effective opponent of President Johnson's policy in Vietnam. Johnson had forced through Congress the greatest legislation in the history of the civil rights movement. He had done this at great personal risk, persuading Southern Democrats to support legislation they had always opposed in the past. King's decision to attack the war was a turning point in Johnson's loss of his liberal political base. He never forgave King for this act of 'betrayal'.

Listen to Martin Luther King's speech for yourself: search YouTube for 'King speech Riverside Church'

Black Power

After the Civil Rights and Voting Rights Acts, King found it more difficult to maintain his commitment to non-violence. To a certain extent he was the victim of his own success. Now that the US Government had outlawed segregation, racial discrimination and the disenfranchisement of black Americans, the arguments were moving into more complex and difficult territory. Blacks were demanding better housing and employment. Some were already calling for 'affirmative action', or 'positive discrimination', to favour black job applicants over whites. These were much more difficult targets than the straight moral issues of the 1950s, and King found them hard to deal with. How could he, who had always fought discrimination, now demand that employers and colleges should discriminate in favour of blacks?

By 1965 the civil rights movement had divided into two broad factions. On the one hand, the non-violent civil disobedience tactics of Martin Luther King and his followers continued to enjoy support, particularly in the South. Inspired by Gandhi's example, the tactics of non-violence drew on traditional Christian values, forcing America to examine its collective conscience about racial issues. But King repeatedly warned American politicians that time was running out if they wanted to avoid an upsurge in violence.

From the mid-1960s the frustration and anger of blacks in the ghettos of northern industrial cities boiled over into riots and violence. Black Power rejected Christianity as a white man's religion. The Nation of Islam, led by Elijah Mohammed, promoted Islam as an African faith more suited to the descendants of African slaves. Malcolm X rejected the 'slave name' of his ancestors. He argued that it was inevitable that the violence of white society towards blacks would be met with violence. He denied that he was an instigator of violence – it was America's white society, he said, that was responsible for this.

After 1965 the Black Power movement became even more forthright in its approach to violence. Stokely Carmichael, the new leader of the **SNCC**, called on black Americans to reject integration and embrace a self-imposed segregation. He accused white America of unremitting racism, exterminating the American Indians and waging war in Vietnam against coloured people (the 'gooks', 'dinks' or 'slopes' of American military slang). The disproportionate number of black Americans drafted into the war drew attention to the poverty and poor educational opportunities of young black American men. Many black Americans refused to fight the Vietnamese when they believed the real war – the struggle for black rights – was being fought in the United States.

The Black Panthers were the most visible sign of the Black Power movement. Armed and dressed in black paramilitary uniforms, they were accused of murdering white policemen and of encouraging blacks to arm themselves. In 1965 the Watts district of Los Angeles was devastated by a race riot in which 23 people were killed. In the 'long hot summers' from 1966 to 1969 riots spread across the cities of America, especially northern industrial cities like Chicago, Detroit and Philadelphia. When Martin Luther King was assassinated in Memphis, Tennessee in 1968, riots affected nearly all cities with sizeable black ghettos. It seemed that efforts to improve racial harmony were failing in the face of poverty, hatred and war.

Malcolm X was assassinated in 1965 for criticising Elijah Mohammed and withdrawing from the movement. He became disenchanted with Elijah Mohammed when he learned that his leader was abusing his fame and position to sexually abuse young women. He also grew to oppose the promotion of violence, as opposed to justifying violence in response to violence.

SNCC
Student Non-Violent Coordinating Committee.

Watch Stokely Carmichael's speech 'Surviving America' by searching for it on YouTube.

An extended interview with Malcolm X at UC Berkeley can be found on YouTube.

The case of Muhammad Ali

Muhammad Ali was perhaps the greatest boxer in history. In 1960 he won a gold medal at the Olympic Games. In 1963 he defeated Sonny Liston to become the WBA World Heavyweight Champion. Ali's path to glory was not easy. In 1964, after being refused service in a whites-only restaurant, he threw his Olympic gold medal into the Ohio River. Born Cassius Clay, he joined the Nation of Islam. By rejecting Christianity and his 'slave name', Ali was asserting his African identity over his American background, a move that made him unpopular with many white Americans. By joining the Nation of Islam, Ali was also rejecting the leadership of Martin Luther King. As Ali once said, 'We who follow the teachings of Elijah Mohammed don't want to be forced to integrate. Integration is wrong. … No intelligent black man or black woman in his or her right mind wants white boys and girls coming to their homes to marry their black sons and daughters.'

What he did next angered white America even more, and turned Ali into a black American hero. In 1966 he received his draft papers for the Army. When he was called up, Ali refused the draft. 'I ain't got no quarrel with them Viet Cong,' he said. 'They never called me nigger.'

Ali paid dearly for his decision. He was arrested, found guilty of refusing military service and sentenced to five years' imprisonment. Worse still, he was stripped of his world heavyweight title – so when he got out of jail, he had to win it all over again. He did this in a series of fights that culminated in a famous contest with George Foreman in Zaire ('the Rumble in the Jungle').

△ **Muhammad Ali having just refused the draft.**

■ Concluding your enquiry

1 Look back over the notes you have made about each of the four issues you have studied – the student movement, the economy, politics, the civil rights movement. For each issue you should now have answered three questions.

2 Use this information to construct a diagram like the one opposite. Any changes that you think were caused solely by the Vietnam War should go in the centre circle. Changes that you think were greatly influenced by the war but not entirely due to Vietnam should go in the middle circle. In the outer circle, place those changes that you think had little to do with the Vietnam War.

Changes that had little to do with the Vietnam War

Changes greatly influenced by the Vietnam War

Changes caused solely by the Vietnam War

3 Use the completed diagram to plan an answer to the enquiry question, 'What impact did the Vietnam War have on America?'

And finally … what do I think?

The student movement and the civil rights movement both began before American combat troops were sent to Vietnam. The main economic changes described in this chapter would have happened regardless. Similarly, once President Johnson and Congress had passed civil rights legislation, I do not think the 'solid Democratic South' could have survived, or the drift to the right in American politics been prevented. On the surface, then, the Vietnam War would appear to have had a minimal impact.

Yet nothing could be further from the truth. The Vietnam War certainly destroyed Lyndon Johnson's presidency. It also acted as a catalyst, increasing the speed and the intensity of the cultural and political changes occurring at that time. It gave these issues an added urgency by suggesting that problems could be solved by force. Conscription ensured that the whole of American youth was involved in the national argument. In 1969 the voting age was lowered from 21 to 18 – if a man was old enough to fight for his country, he was old enough to vote.

The Vietnam War was responsible for a deep malaise running through American society at this time. We can narrow down the period in which this occurred to the years 1968–72. In these years America's young people experienced a kind of nihilism – the pointlessness of all things. The slow, religious world into which the 'baby boomer' generation was born was collapsing. Nothing seemed to have meaning, purpose or value. The experience of being trapped in a war America could not win or abandon induced a national pessimism that expressed itself in destructive, and self-destructive, behaviour. Even the presidency was affected: the Watergate Affair was deeply influenced by the war in Vietnam, starting with Nixon's attempt to discredit Daniel Ellsberg, the man who released the **Pentagon Papers**. It contributed to Nixon's paranoia; by the time he left office in 1974, Nixon regarded antiwar protestors as the 'enemy within'.

It is interesting to note how America calmed down when the war ended. The 'long hot summers' – the most destructive period of riots in modern American history – coincided precisely with the escalation of the war in Vietnam, 1965–69. The last American combat troops withdrew from Vietnam in 1973. By this time the worst of the student protests, race riots and political violence were over. The next generation of students were more conservative, interested more in their careers than they were in politics or social justice.

Pentagon Papers
A secret government document commissioned by Robert McNamara in 1966 to find out how the war had started. Daniel Ellsberg smuggled the document out of the Pentagon and gave it to the *New York Times*, which published it in 1970.

Were these the photographs that lost the war?

As discussed in Chapter 3, both orthodox and revisionist historians have argued that the antiwar movement forced America out of Vietnam. This claim has been disputed, but there is no doubt that photo-journalism played a major role in forcing Americans to question America's involvement.

In Vietnam the press was given almost unlimited access to the conflict. Many Americans believe that this free access turned the public against the war. This has led the US Government to place much stricter controls on journalists in recent conflicts in Kuwait, Iraq and Afghanistan.

On the other hand, it is also argued that America had a right to know what was going on. Unlike its Cold War adversaries, America held the freedom of the press to be a fundamental liberty, enshrined in the constitution. Just as America did not cover up the failures in its space programme, neither did it cover up the reality of what was happening in Vietnam.

As you look at each image, consider why the photograph is so powerful.

△ My Lai, 16 March 1968. Photographer: Ronald Haeberle, US Army. A group of women and children about to be killed by American soldiers. Haeberle was carrying two cameras that day, an Army camera and his own personal one. On the camera issued by the US Army he recorded mostly standard images of operations. On his personal camera he photographed the massacre as it unfolded. The *New York Times* published his pictures 'as a matter of public interest'.

▽ Kent State University, Ohio, 4 May 1970. Photographer: John Filo. The picture shows Mary Ann Vecchio kneeling over the body of Jeffrey Miller, who has just been shot dead by the National Guard.

◁ My Lai, 16 March 1968. Photographer: Ronald Haeberle. The aftermath of the My Lai massacre.

△ 'Reaching Out', Mutter Ridge, Niu Cay Tri, 5 October 1966. Photographer: Larry Burrows. This picture was taken at a casualty clearing station south of the DMZ. It shows Marine gunnery sergeant Jeremiah Purdie moving to comfort a badly wounded comrade.

◁ Nguyen Ngoc Loan, South Vietnam's Chief of National Police, executing Nguyen Van Len, a suspected Viet Cong guerrilla, 1 February 1968. Photographer: Eddie Adams. According to the veteran war photographer Don McCullin, 'More even than the My Lai massacre, that picture was to create a turning point in the heart of the American people.'

▷ Phan Thi Kim Phuc running from her village after being struck by napalm, 8 June 1972. Photographer: Huynh Cong Ut. Huynh Cong Ut dropped to one knee, putting his camera at the children's level. That is why this particular picture, of several taken at that moment, was the one that caught the world's attention.

Popular music and the Vietnam War

This was the war of the rock 'n' roll era. Popular music provided the war poetry of the Vietnam era. Pop music itself was changing very rapidly, with various styles like Motown, hard rock, heavy metal, folk rock and pop competing for attention. In the popular music of the era you can detect changes in the way the public felt about war in general, and this war in particular.

The following tracks all contain references to the war in Vietnam. Download them and listen to the lyrics to get the feel of the times. The final four tracks are more modern songs that look back on the war from a more recent perspective.

1 *The Ballad of the Green Berets*, 1965 – Sgt Barry Sadler. Catches the early patriotism near the start of the war.

2 *I Feel Like I'm a Fixin' to Die*, 1965 – Country Joe and the Fish. Catches the early cynicism.

3 *Lyndon Johnson Told the Nation*, 1965 – Tom Paxton. A folk protest song that revealed early disquiet at events in Vietnam.

4 *Galveston*, 1969 – Glen Campbell. Expresses the loneliness of soldiers far from home.

5 *Ruby Don't Take Your Love to Town*, 1969 – Kenny Rogers. 'It wasn't me that started that old crazy Asian war…'

6 *Fortunate Son*, 1969 – Creedence Clearwater Revival. A hard rock protest song that caught the anger of those who had to fight on behalf of those who managed to escape from it.

7 *The Star Spangled Banner*, 1969 – Jimi Hendrix. Recorded at the Woodstock Festival, Hendrix comments on the distorted patriotism of the flag-waving brigade.

8 *Gimme Shelter*, 1969 – The Rolling Stones. British, admittedly, but the Stones managed to catch the mood of a world gone to hell.

9 *War*, 1970 – Edwin Starr. 'What is it good for? Absolutely nothing!'

10 *Give Peace A Chance*, 1970 – John Lennon and The Plastic Ono Band. Probably the most famous antiwar song of the era.

11 *Ohio*, 1970 – Crosby, Stills, Nash & Young. Written after the deaths of four students at Kent State University, Ohio.

12 *What's Going On*, 1972 – Marvin Gaye. The gentlest expression of dismay at the waste of life in Vietnam.

14 *The Grave*, 1971 – Don McLean. When I first heard this, I thought it must be about the Second World War – we couldn't possibly be sacrificing Marines in the 1970s!

15 *Goodnight Saigon*, 1982 – Billy Joel. If one song can summarise America's experience in Vietnam, this is it.

16 *Born in the USA*, 1984 – Bruce Springsteen. President Reagan thought this song was pro-American. Did he hear the words?

17 *Orange Crush*, 1988 – REM. Typical REM song that never quite says what is on their mind. Orange Crush is Agent Orange.

18 *Deja Vu (All Over Again)*, 2004 – John Fogerty. As public opinion turned against the Iraq War, John Fogerty reminded his audience that they had heard it all before.

4 Why did the USA get involved in the Vietnam War?

> The road to hell is paved with good intentions.
>
> Old proverb

The official government view during the war was that America was fighting to defend South Vietnam from communist aggression. The USA saw South Vietnam as an independent country whose freedom was under attack. If South Vietnam fell, the USA feared other countries in Southeast Asia would follow.

However, if that view was largely accepted at first, it was challenged as the war went on. In 1967 Martin Luther King attacked the Vietnam War:

> We are adding cynicism to the process of death, for [American soldiers] must know after a short period that none of the things we claim to be fighting for are really involved.
>
> Martin Luther King, 'A Time to Break Silence', 4 April 1967

To understand why Martin Luther King and many others were so critical of the USA's involvement in Vietnam we need to understand the values that America stood for. In 1945, at the end of the Second World War, millions of people saw America as the greatest force for good in the world. Twice, in 1917 and in 1941, the United States had come to the aid of countries threatened by aggression. It was not only Americans who believed this: millions of people in Europe, Asia and Africa looked to America for leadership. Even Ho Chi Minh believed this: in 1945 he quoted **Thomas Jefferson** in Vietnam's declaration of independence from France. What did America stand for in 1945?

Thomas Jefferson
The principal author of the American Declaration of Independence.

1   **Freedom.** In 1776 America declared independence from Great Britain. Anticolonialism was a byword for American freedom. In 1823 America declared its hostility to any European power that tried to interfere with the New World, a policy known as the Monroe Doctrine. In 1916 President Wilson declared that national self-determination – the right of people to govern themselves – was a basic American principle. During the Second World War President Roosevelt made it clear that America would not assist European countries to retain or regain control over their former territories.

2   **Democracy.** American politics are decided through democratic elections. In 1919 the franchise was extended to women, and although many black Americans were still denied the vote in practice, in theory every American citizen was entitled to vote and every vote was of equal value. The Bill of Rights protected certain freedoms that were necessary for democracy to work – freedom of the press, freedom of assembly, freedom of speech, freedom of religion and the right to a fair trial.

3   **The Constitution.** The American Constitution established 'a government of laws, not men', in which politics had to obey certain rules. By separating the powers of the president, Congress and the Supreme Court, and through a system of checks and balances, the Constitution aimed to prevent power being concentrated in the hands of a few people, particularly the president. For example, the president is commander-in-chief of the armed forces, but Congress must declare war, and Congress controls the funding needed to fight wars. In theory, therefore, the United States was a force for peace – slow to anger, its policies determined not by a single individual but by the will of the people.

Following these principles might seem straightforward, but the United States was not operating in a historical vacuum after 1945. The Cold War created new problems, forcing American presidents to make decisions that often conflicted with the principles outlined above. One such decision was to send American troops to South Vietnam, a country that would not have existed if promised elections had been held, to support a dictator who denied his people basic human rights. Such an intervention seemed to be against the very principles the USA stood for. How did this happen?

■ **Enquiry Focus:** Why did the USA get involved in the Vietnam War?

This chapter is built around four critical decisions taken by the US Government between 1945 and 1965. In each case, events were moving quickly and the president faced difficult choices. Each decision had consequences that altered the history of Vietnam. It could be argued that, step by step, the United States abandoned its basic principles, with terrible consequences for both the Vietnamese and the American people.

As you work through this chapter you will encounter each of these four critical decisions in turn.

1 For each decision (numbered 1 to 4 on the timeline) make detailed notes outlining:

    a) the choices the president faced

    b) the decision the president made, and why he chose this option

    c) the consequences of that decision.

Cold War timeline	Vietnam War timeline
Allied victory in Second World War, 1945	**1945** ① Should America help to restore French control in Indochina? (Roosevelt and Truman)
Truman Doctrine Marshall Plan Berlin Blockade COLD WAR BEGINNING IN EUROPE NATO formed, 1949 Chinese civil war won by communists, 1949 USSR explodes its first atomic bomb, 1950 North Korea invades South Korea, 1950 KOREAN WAR, 1950–53 Stalin's death, 1953	**1950** VIET MINH FIGHT WAR OF INDEPENDENCE FROM FRANCE, 1945–54
Battle of Dine Bien Phu, 1954 Warsaw Pact formed, 1955	**1955** ② Should America support the Geneva Accord on the future of Vietnam? (Eisenhower)
Khrushchev emerges as Soviet premier 'Space race' begins with Sputnik, 1957	
Cuban Revolution, 1959 U2 incident, 1960 Berlin Wall built, 1961 Cuban Missile Crisis, 1962	**1960** ③ Should America send military advisors to support the South Vietnamese Army? (Kennedy)
Brezhnev replaces Khrushchev in USSR, 1965	**1965** ④ Gulf of Tonkin incident. Should America commit combat troops to help defend South Vietnam? (Johnson)

△ The road to Vietnam.

2 The mind map below shows the major factors driving America towards war. After making your notes, annotate your copy of this mind map to record evidence of the impact of each factor.

The domino theory   American prestige

Factors driving America towards war

Fear of domestic criticism   Cold War rhetoric

You will find a concluding activity on page 75.

The domino theory. Did American presidents believe that the defence of South Vietnam was essential to the freedom and independence of other countries in Southeast Asia?

American prestige. Did America get drawn into Vietnam because no president could admit that his predecessor had made a mistake?

Fear of domestic criticism. Did American presidents choose to get more and more deeply involved in Vietnam for fear of what their political opponents would say if they chose to back off?

Cold War rhetoric. Did American presidents get trapped by their own pronouncements and promises, forcing them to take action or lose their credibility?

Decision 1: 1945: Should America help to restore French control in Indochina?

a) The context

The Vietnamese were fighting long before American troops got involved. Their war began in 1941 when the Japanese occupied Indochina and continued when France tried to restore its control after Japan's defeat in 1945. To understand America's dilemma, we need to know something about Vietnam's experience of French rule.

The French empire in Indochina dated back to the 1880s, a time when most European countries were establishing colonies in Asia and Africa. The French claimed that theirs was a 'civilising mission', bringing French culture, Catholicism, investments, law and order to Vietnam. In reality few Vietnamese benefited from French rule. A Vietnamese elite collaborated with the French, adopting French manners, language and religion, in return for education, land and economic privileges. Vietnam was a market for French produce, and it exported raw materials profitable or helpful to French industry, especially rice, silk and rubber. Large rubber plantations, owned by French companies, concentrated land ownership in the hands of a privileged elite, leaving most Vietnamese peasants as landless sharecroppers. The French made little effort to improve the standard of living in their colonies. Compared with the American protectorate in the Philippines, where there was one doctor for every 3,000 local inhabitants, the French provided only one doctor for every 38,000 Vietnamese. President Roosevelt regarded Vietnam as the worst example of European colonialism.

During the Second World War both France and the French colonial administration in Vietnam had to endure the humiliation of defeat:

- In May 1940 the German blitzkrieg inflicted a crushing defeat on France. The psychological impact of this defeat was profound.

- Hitler's victory divided the French people. The German Army occupied northern France. A collaborating French government known as the Vichy regime governed southern France. France's colonies – including Vietnam – continued under Vichy administration on the proviso that they stayed out of the war.

- In September 1940 the Japanese invaded French Indochina. After token resistance the French gave in, and then collaborated with the Japanese by continuing to administer Vietnam on Japan's behalf. Japan's invasion of Indochina had two important consequences for the future of Southeast Asia:
  - The Americans placed an oil embargo on Japan. This led to the Japanese attack on Pearl Harbor in December 1941 and the Pacific War that followed (see Section 2).
  - The Viet Minh formed in May 1941 to fight against the Japanese occupation, beginning a war of national liberation against both the Japanese and the French.

b) The dilemma

By 1945 President Roosevelt faced an uncomfortable choice. For four years the Viet Minh had fought the Japanese, assisted by the Americans. The Organisation of Strategic Services (OSS) sent weapons and medical supplies to resistance groups in Indochina, encouraging guerrilla warfare to tie down Japanese forces. On 2 September 1945 Japan surrendered to the Allies. One week later, the Viet Minh declared independence from France, and warned France not to attempt to resume control over Vietnam. The Viet Minh looked to the United States to support Vietnamese independence by refusing to support the French. If America stood for freedom, now was the time to stand up for its principles.

France was determined to regain its former colonies. Restoring French sovereignty in Vietnam would help restore national pride after the humiliations endured during the war. The French appealed to President Roosevelt to provide ships to transport French forces to Indochina. Roosevelt stalled, hoping to persuade France to agree to act as a trustee and prepare Indochina for independence. The French were having none of it. The issue was so divisive that the future of Indochina was not discussed at the **Yalta conference** in February 1945.

The dilemma was this: should America help France regain control in Vietnam? Or should the USA help the Vietnamese gain independence from France?

c) The decision

The sudden death of President Roosevelt in April 1945 removed the most important block on French ambitions in Vietnam. His successor, President Truman, was far less concerned about French colonialism than about the spread of communism. Already the Soviet Union was putting communists into power in those parts of eastern Europe it had liberated from the Nazis – the beginning of what became known as the 'Iron Curtain'.

Truman was coming under pressure from France and Britain to restore their colonial empires. America needed their support in Europe to resist the spread of communism, so France warned the USA that French support for America in Europe depended on American support for France in Indochina. Britain, fearful for the future of British India, Burma, Malaya and Singapore, supported French demands for colonial restoration.

There were also divisions within the US administration. The State Department was divided between the Europeanists, who wanted French support against the growing Soviet threat, and the Far Eastern desk, which encouraged decolonisation and independence, not only in Indochina but in India, the Dutch East Indies, Malaya and the Philippines.

Faced with a choice between supporting the Viet Minh or the French, the Americans chose the French. The United States would help France to regain its former colony in Indochina. This was brought home by the Japanese surrender in Vietnam: north of the 17th parallel, the Japanese surrendered to Chiang Kai-shek's nationalist Chinese. In the south the Japanese surrendered to the British, who promptly rearmed the Japanese Army to prevent disorder (i.e. to prevent a Viet Minh victory) until the

Yalta conference
The Allied conference held in the Crimea and attended by President Roosevelt, Winston Churchill and Josef Stalin. The aim of the conference was to begin planning for the post-war world.

French Army could take over. Two French divisions duly arrived on American ships, fully equipped by the United States. These events were seared into Vietnamese national consciousness – it was clear that they could never trust the Western powers.

d) The consequences

Why did the Americans choose France over the Viet Minh? They did so because the pressure to restore French colonialism proved irresistible because of the fear of communism and the assumption – encouraged by the French – that Ho Chi Minh and the Viet Minh were Soviet stooges. It was a question of priorities – as long as America got French support against the Soviet Union in Europe, the future of Vietnam was of little account. The Americans hoped that France would reform its administration in Vietnam and prepare the country for independence. In the meantime, they had to ensure that France regained control of Vietnam successfully.

In 1946 the Viet Minh launched their war of national liberation against the French. The war lasted eight years, ending with the French defeat at the Battle of Dien Bien Phu. During those years, the Americans became more and more convinced that preventing a communist victory in Vietnam was essential to America's own security. The domino theory had become universally accepted in American policy-making circles. The closer France came to defeat, the more frantic the American efforts to support the French became.

△ The domino theory.

1 For America's first big decision about Vietnam, make detailed notes outlining:
   a) the choices Presidents Roosevelt and Truman faced
   b) the decision that President Truman made
   c) the consequences of that decision: how Truman's decision affected the future of Vietnam
   d) why America decided to help restore French colonialism, when the USA had opposed this during the Second World War.

2 On your own copy of the mind map, summarise your findings to create a visual summary of your detailed notes.

Decision 2: 1954: Should America support the Geneva Accord on the future of Vietnam?

a) The context

The late 1940s and 1950s were dominated by the onset of the Cold War:

- 1946: Churchill's 'Iron Curtain' speech in Fulton, Missouri, warned the Americans of the growing threat of communism in eastern Europe.
- 1946: The Truman Doctrine. President Truman committed the United States to a policy of containment to halt the spread of communism.
- 1947: Marshall Plan for the economic regeneration of Europe. The economic recovery of western Europe would help to prevent the spread of communism.
- 1948: Berlin Blockade and Airlift – the first major confrontation of the Cold War, when the Soviet Union blockaded West Berlin and the Western powers airlifted supplies until the Soviet Union backed down.
- 1949: The USSR developed its own atomic bomb. America was now threatened with nuclear weapons.
- 1949: West Germany created as a separate state – this marked the end of hopes for German reunification.
- 1949: NATO alliance established to protect western Europe and North America from a possible Soviet attack.
- 1953: America and the USSR develop the hydrogen bomb, a much more powerful nuclear weapon.

The 'failure' of containment in Asia

In the late 1940s and early 1950s the Truman Doctrine of containment suffered a series of setbacks that had serious effects on American domestic politics:

- 1945–47: Marshall mission to China. A diplomatic mission to try to find a peaceful solution to the Chinese civil war. General George C. Marshall tried and failed to prevent a communist victory.
- 1949: China became communist with the victory of Mao Zedong's communist forces over Chiang Kai-shek's nationalists.
- 1950: North Korea invaded South Korea. The UN sent an army to defend South Korea under American command. In 1951 China entered the war on North Korea's side. For the next two years American and Chinese forces fought each other to a standstill, ending with an armistice in July 1953.

The McCarthy era in America

Senator Joseph McCarthy led an anticommunist 'witch hunt' in America in the early 1950s. The communist victory in China, together with the outbreak of the Korean War, was a toxic combination that led to political and moral panic in the United States – the Red Scare and the McCarthy era. McCarthy focused his political attack on events in Asia.

- 1947: Hollywood Ten directors and producers blacklisted for refusing to testify before the House Committee of Un-American Activities.
- 1948: Alger Hiss case. Hiss was convicted of perjury under suspicion of having passed secret information to the USSR during the Second World War.
- 1950: McCarran Internal Security Act – members of communist organisations required to register with the government and barred from holding US passports or working in defence industries.
- 1950: McCarthy claims to have a list of over 200 communists working in the US State Department, where they could undermine American foreign policy.
- 1951: Julius and Ethel Rosenberg found guilty of passing atomic secrets to the Russians. Executed for treason in 1953.
- 1951: General George C. Marshall attacked by McCarthy for the failure of the Marshall mission to China. McCarthy accused Marshall of making decisions that 'aided the communist drive for world domination'.
- 1954: Army–McCarthy hearings in the Senate. McCarthy accused the US Army of containing suspected communists and security risks. He was really blaming the Army for failing to defeat the communists in the Korean War.

The Army–McCarthy hearings exposed McCarthy as a fraudulent demagogue, and soon the Senate censured his conduct, which ended his reign of influence. Nevertheless, the febrile atmosphere created by McCarthyism continued to have a powerful impact on US policy.

b) The dilemma

In 1954 President Eisenhower faced a new dilemma. After eight years of fighting, the French decided to pull out of Vietnam. At the same time there was a gradual improvement in East–West relations following the death of Stalin in 1953. The Soviet foreign minister, Molotov, suggested an international conference to discuss the future of Indochina. The main countries at the conference were France, the United States, the Soviet Union, communist China and Great Britain, with delegates also from Laos, Cambodia, the **Associated States of Vietnam** and the Viet Minh. The meeting was held in Geneva in April 1954 and produced an accord, or blueprint, for the resolution of the crisis.

Associated States of Vietnam
A 'puppet government' for Vietnam established by France in 1949 to give the impression that France was allowing the Vietnamese people to govern themselves.

Geneva Accord, 1954

- An immediate ceasefire
- Laos and Cambodia to become independent states
- Vietnam divided temporarily into North and South along the 17th parallel
- An International Control Commission to supervise the implementation of these terms
- Nationwide elections to be held throughout Vietnam by July 1956, followed by reunification
- French forces to remain until asked to leave by the Associated States

The dilemma was this: should America support the Geneva Accord, and take the risk that Vietnam would choose a communist government? Or should the USA help South Vietnam become an independent, non-communist state?

c) The decision

America did not support the Geneva Accord. The Viet Minh were the only popular, organised group in Vietnam – if elections were held in 1956, the communists would win. Democracy would produce an outcome unacceptable to the United States. Therefore when the French pulled out, the Americans helped to create a country called 'South Vietnam' and pledged to defend it.

The decision not to support the 1954 Geneva Accord was heavily influenced by domestic political considerations. To 'lose' Vietnam to communism after 'losing' China would be political suicide. The 1952 presidential election returned a Republican administration heavily influenced by right-wing anticommunists and by the China Lobby, the group of businessmen and politicians most committed to the exiled nationalist government in Taiwan. The new secretary of state, John Foster Dulles, was determined that the Geneva Conference would fail. Dulles feared that the communist victory in China was the beginning of a 'domino effect' that would undermine America's position in the Far East if left unchecked. More than this, Dulles believed that Truman's containment policy was not sufficient. He believed that American policy should aim at rolling back communism in China itself, by force if necessary. Many Americans agreed with Dulles that Truman and the Democrats had badly mishandled the crisis in the Far East since 1945, and wanted to see a much more aggressive strategy.

Learning trouble spot: How American foreign policy is made

The process of making foreign policy in America is quite complicated. The State Department is the official government department responsible for foreign relations, but as we have seen, it was divided into factions, the Europeanists and the Far Eastern desk, working for different outcomes. The Senate Foreign Relations Committee leads foreign-policy legislation in Congress and confirms the president's nominations for high-level positions in the State Department. The president, advised by his White House staff, has the final word in making foreign policy.

The Cold War forced the US Government to add several new layers to this original structure. The National Security Council (NSC) was created in 1947: it is the forum that gathers the various agency heads together with the president to advise and assist his decision-making. The Central Intelligence Agency (CIA) was also formed in 1947 to gather intelligence about foreign governments and carry out covert operations. The National Security Agency (NSA) was formed in 1952 for collecting, decoding, translating and analysing signals intelligence from foreign countries.

Throughout the Cold War it was quite common for specialists from the State Department to advise one thing, while the NSC advised something else. Most State Department employees are professional career diplomats, whereas the NSC consists mostly of political appointees more immediately influenced by public opinion.

d) The consequences

The immediate consequence of America's refusal to support the 1954 Geneva Accord was that Vietnam was split in two. In the North a communist Viet Minh government was formed under the leadership of Ho Chi Minh and General Giap, the commander who had defeated the French. In the South, a new unelected government was formed under the premiership of Ngo Dinh Diem. Diem seemed an ideal leader of South Vietnam; a nationalist who had opposed French control, he opposed communism and promised social reform.

---

1 For America's second big decision about Vietnam, make detailed notes outlining:

a) the choice President Eisenhower faced

b) the decision that Eisenhower made

c) the consequences of that decision: how Eisenhower's decision affected the future of Vietnam

d) why America prevented the democratic elections scheduled for July 1956 under the Geneva Accord.

2 On your own copy of the mind map, summarise your findings to create a visual summary of your detailed notes. Note in particular the role played in this decision by domestic political pressures in the United States.

Decision 3: 1961: Should America send military advisors to support the South Vietnamese Army?

a) The context

John F. Kennedy won the 1960 presidential election by the narrowest margin of the twentieth century, winning just 100,000 votes more than his Republican rival, Richard Nixon. This meant that Kennedy was politically vulnerable so, to balance his liberal domestic agenda, he had to show that he was tough on communism, especially as he had criticised his predecessor, President Eisenhower, for falling behind the Soviet Union in the race to develop nuclear missiles. In his inaugural address in January 1961 Kennedy reaffirmed America's commitment to the **Truman Doctrine**.

Kennedy was aware of the challenges America faced in the 1960s, and he was determined to rise to them. In the first year of his presidency he faced several Cold War crises. Two of the most significant were:

Truman Doctrine
The policy that committed the United States to containing the spread of communism.

■ The Bay of Pigs fiasco, 1961. This was an operation Kennedy inherited from Eisenhower, and it went badly wrong. The United States encouraged a small army of Cuban exiles opposed to Castro to invade Cuba at the Bay of Pigs. Kennedy refused to give them direct American military support, and the communists defeated the invasion. It made Kennedy look weak.

■ The Berlin Wall, 1961. East Germany, encouraged by the Soviet Union, built a wall around West Berlin. Kennedy flew to Berlin and made a speech affirming America's determination to stand beside its allies to prevent any further expansion of communism.

In his speeches Kennedy frequently used rhetoric that painted an image of America as the lonely guardian of world freedom against the communist enemy, as this speech, given to the 3rd Armored Division in Germany, on 25 June 1963, shows:

> Stretching all around the globe, there are Americans on duty who help maintain the freedom of dozens of countries who might now be engulfed if it were not for this long thin line which occupies such a position of responsibility, guarding so many gates, where the enemy campfires in some cases can be seen from the top of the wall.

At no point did he really question the assumption that all communist movements the world over were orchestrated from Moscow.

b) The dilemma

In 1959 the communists had formed the National Liberation Front and encouraged communist refugees from South Vietnam – the Viet Cong – to return to the South and launch a guerrilla war, aided by the North Vietnamese Army, which was supplied by the Russians and the Chinese. Under that pressure, South Vietnam might collapse if left to its own devices, especially as the president, Ngo Dinh Diem, was unpopular. The whole of Vietnam might be reunited under communist rule.

The dilemma was this: what could America do, short of war, to prevent the collapse of South Vietnam? Should military advisors be sent to support the South Vietnamese Army?

c) The decision

Kennedy's decision to send military advisors in 1961 did not seem too hard to make, given the commitment of previous American presidents to support South Vietnam's independence. He stepped up American support for South Vietnam by sending military advisers to help train and command the ARVN. Many South Vietnamese officers now had an American officer at their elbow, telling them what to do. This was a major step, because America was taking control of the levers of the conflict. It would be hard to allow South Vietnam to lose the war once American prestige was directly involved. But as he had not sent combat troops, Kennedy could still plausibly deny that this was America's war.

Kennedy also met the new threat of communist uprisings by forming the Special Forces – the Green Berets – as a highly trained counter-insurgency force. The Cold War was to be fought not with large American armies, but with counter-insurgency, covert operations, economic aid and skilful diplomacy.

d) The consequences

By the time Kennedy was assassinated in November 1963 there were 16,000 American military advisers in South Vietnam. Many of these were engaged in a direct combat role, giving orders to American aircraft, advising South Vietnamese officers and planning military operations. The United States was pouring military aid into South Vietnam, alongside the schools and medical supplies of the hearts and minds programme. Covert operations were already under way, including the CIA's Air America programme that used 'civilian' pilots to fly combat missions, not only in Vietnam but in Laos and Cambodia too.

However, by the end of 1963 some of these advisers were already warning the Pentagon that the policy was failing. They were frustrated with the South Vietnamese Government, corruption and the ARVN's unwillingness to fight. They warned that something had to change. Two weeks before Kennedy's assassination, President Ngo Dinh Diem was overthrown and murdered in a military coup that had the tacit approval of the CIA.

1 For America's third big decision about Vietnam, make detailed notes outlining:

   a) the choice President Kennedy faced

   b) the decision that Kennedy made, and why he made it

   c) the consequences of that decision: how Kennedy's decision affected the future of Vietnam.

2 Annotate your mind map to summarise which factors influenced the US decision to send military advisers to Vietnam.

Decision 4: 1964–65: Should America commit combat troops to help defend South Vietnam?

a) The context

Kennedy's assassination, and the overthrow and murder of Ngo Dinh Diem, changed the political situation faced by, and within, the United States. It would have been very difficult for Kennedy's successor, President Johnson, to withdraw from Vietnam. Nobody would have understood why he had done it. When the South fell to the communists, Johnson would get the blame.

In South Vietnam the overthrow of President Diem did nothing to stop the rot. The following conversation between Johnson and Robert McNamara, from 9 June 1964, shows them wrestling with their dilemma:

McNamara: If you went to the CIA and said, 'How is the situation today in South Vietnam?', I think they would say it's worse. You see it in the desertion rate, you see it in the morale, you see it in the difficulty to recruit people, you see it in the gradual loss of population control. Many of us in private would say that things are not good, they've gotten worse. Now while we say this in private and not public, there are facts available that find their way in the press. If we're going to stay in there, if we're going to go up the escalation chain, we're going to have to educate the people, Mr President. We haven't done so yet. I'm not sure now is exactly the right time.

Johnson: No, and I think if you start doing it they're going to be hollering, 'You're a warmonger.'

One recent development of great importance was the Cuban Missile Crisis of 1962, the greatest crisis of the Cold War. The Soviet Union had placed nuclear missiles on Cuba, ostensibly to deter another Bay of Pigs-style invasion, but Khrushchev's ulterior motive was to place America under a direct, immediate nuclear threat. Over two weeks of intense diplomacy and military threats, Kennedy had narrowly avoided nuclear war and persuaded the Russians to remove their missiles with the promise that the United States would not invade Cuba. While war had been avoided, fears of the communist threat had grown even greater. It was particularly important to President Johnson to prove that he was just as resolute and determined as Kennedy had been.

b) The dilemma

During 1964 the situation in South Vietnam continued to get worse. If the country was to be saved, American forces would have to intervene, but Johnson was hoping to avoid a land war in Asia that he knew would be unpopular. Throughout 1964 he discussed the problem with his secretary of defence, McNamara and other advisers. Johnson was very reluctant to send troops to Vietnam, but he was unwilling to allow South Vietnam to fall to the communists. Here is one brief extract from a conversation between Johnson and McGeorge Bundy, his national security advisor, on 27 May 1964:

> It looks to me like we're getting into another Korea. It just worries the hell out of me. I don't see what we can ever hope to get out of there with, once we're committed … I don't think it's worth fighting for and I don't think that we can get out. It's just the biggest damned mess that I ever saw.

The dilemma was this: should America send combat troops to Vietnam? If it did not, South Vietnam was likely to fall.

c) The decision: The war that was not supposed to happen

During the 1964 presidential election Johnson made it clear that he did not intend to get drawn into a war in Vietnam. 'We don't want our American boys to do the fighting for Asian boys. We don't want to get involved in a nation with 700 million people and get tied down in a land war in Asia.' Johnson was duly re-elected in November 1964. On 8 March 1965 the first US combat troops arrived in South Vietnam. So did something happen that forced Johnson to break his promise? Let's look at the events that actually led to war.

I remember the incident that led America into the Vietnam War. We had a big black-and-white TV in my parents' bedroom. Every evening my father came home from work (he was a history teacher) and sat down to have his supper in front of the five o'clock news. On this particular night the news report was shocking. An American destroyer, the USS *Maddox*, had been attacked on the high seas by North Vietnamese torpedo boats! Imagine our surprise – how dare they! Our ship was in international waters, and the communists just attacked it!

Gulf of Tonkin incident, 2–4 August, 1964. On 2 August the USS *Maddox* was attacked by North Vietnamese torpedo boats in the Gulf of Tonkin. Johnson reinforced the *Maddox* with the USS *C. Turner Joy.* Two days later this ship reported itself under attack by North Vietnamese forces.

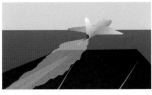

President Johnson's retaliation. Johnson was outraged. This aggression could not go unpunished. He ordered the US Navy to launch punitive air strikes against targets in North Vietnam, and went to Congress to ask for money to defend South Vietnam. Congress passed the Tonkin Gulf Resolution (7 August 1964), allowing Johnson 'to take all necessary steps, including the use of armed force'. Congress surrendered its constitutional authority to declare war by passing this resolution. Only two Senators out of 100 voted against it.

North Vietnam saw the Tonkin Gulf Resolution as a declaration of war by the United States. As a warning to America not to get further involved, the Viet Cong stepped up their attacks on American interests in South Vietnam. On 7 February 1965 the Viet Cong attacked the American airbase at Pleiku, destroying several American aircraft.

One week after the attack on Pleiku, Johnson ordered 'Operation Rolling Thunder' – the sustained bombing of North Vietnam. The object was to avoid having to commit US ground troops to the war in Vietnam.

The Viet Cong attack on Pleiku showed that US airbases in South Vietnam were vulnerable to enemy attack. To protect the large US airfield at Da Nang, Johnson ordered the US Marines to establish a security cordon around the airfield. The Marines landed at Da Nang on 8 March 1965.

To fulfil their mission the Marines at Da Nang began to carry out 'search and destroy' sweeps of the surrounding countryside. Other US units were now arriving to take control of the war from the South Vietnamese.

d) The consequences

Over the next couple of years the war escalated as more and more American troops arrived in South Vietnam. The war had begun in earnest with the arrival of combat troops at Da Nang.

During a Senate debate on Vietnam on 27 May 1964 (nine months before combat troops arrived in Vietnam) Senator Wayne Morse of Oregon had criticised President Johnson for waging an 'undeclared war' in Vietnam. 'The Constitution,' he said, 'still requires a declaration of war or a treaty obligation before American soldiers can be sent into battle, and as the Secretary of Defense knows, American soldiers are now fighting in South Vietnam not under a declaration of war nor in pursuance of a treaty, but on the orders of Mr McNamara. That makes our war illegal under the Constitution of the United States.' The soldiers that Senator Morse was referring to were the military advisers sent by Kennedy to support the South Vietnamese Army, many of whom were Green Beret counter-insurgency forces. It could be argued, therefore, that US combat troops first arrived in Vietnam in 1961.

Two months after this debate the Tonkin Gulf Resolution was passed. It was on this basis that the Vietnam War was fought. Vietnam was a 'presidential war', authorised but largely uncontrolled by Congress. It was the kind of war that the American Constitution tried to avoid by separating the powers at the heart of government (see page 61), but the Cold War in general, and the existence of nuclear weapons in particular, had weakened the constitutional separation of powers and strengthened the authority of the presidency.

The United States has not made any formal declarations of war since 1942, but it has fought wars in Korea, Vietnam, Kuwait, Iraq and Afghanistan. In Korea the war was authorised by the United Nations, to which America had treaty obligations. Formal declarations of war are not a prerequisite to American military action, and many people would argue that they are inappropriate in the modern world of 'police actions' and limited objectives. In this sense, America did not necessarily ignore legal process when it went to war in Vietnam. However, because Congress gave the president full authority to take 'all necessary measures', it gave away its constitutional role of acting as a brake on presidential power. The rapid escalation of the war thereafter was the result of this excessive trust that Congress placed in the president.

---

1 For America's fourth big decision about Vietnam, make detailed notes outlining:

  a) the choice President Johnson faced

  b) the decision that Johnson made and why he made it

  c) the reasons why Congress was willing to trust the president's judgement

  d) the consequences of that decision: the American war in Vietnam and the escalation of the war as more and more troops were committed.

2 Annotate your mind map to summarise which factors influenced the US decision to commit combat troops in Vietnam.

■ Concluding your enquiry

1 Now you need to take a step back and survey the process as a whole. Using your completed chart, consider how important each of these factors was in driving America towards war between 1945 and 1965:

- **The domino theory.** Did these American presidents believe that the defence of South Vietnam was essential to the freedom and independence of other countries in Southeast Asia?

- **American prestige.** Did America get drawn into Vietnam because no president could admit that his predecessor had made a mistake?

- **Fear of domestic criticism.** Did American presidents choose to get more and more deeply involved in Vietnam for fear of what their political opponents would say if they chose to back off?

- **Cold War rhetoric.** Did America become the victim of its own Cold War rhetoric?

2 Now write an essay in answer to the following question: why did the USA get involved in the Vietnam War?

Did the American Government lie about Vietnam?

During the 1964 election President Johnson ran against the Republican candidate, Senator Barry Goldwater. Johnson's campaign presented Goldwater as a warmonger. In a famous TV advert, a little girl counting daisy petals changed into a nuclear countdown, ending in the explosion of a hydrogen bomb. A vote for Johnson, it said, was a vote for peace. Goldwater accused Johnson of lying to the American people. 'Make no bones of this,' he said in August 1964. 'Don't try to sweep this under the rug. We are at war in Vietnam, and yet the president and his secretary of defence continue to mislead and misinform the American people.' Years later he said, 'You see I was being called trigger-happy, warmonger, bomb-happy, and all the time Johnson was saying he would never send American boys, I knew damn well he would.'

In 1971 the *New York Times* published the Pentagon Papers, smuggled out of the Pentagon by Daniel Ellsberg, a strategic analyst who had worked for Robert McNamara. The Pentagon Papers supported Goldwater's accusation that Johnson was already committed to war in Vietnam in 1964.

Johnson therefore stands accused of lying to the American public about his intentions in 1964. According to his public statements during the 1964 election, he had no intention of committing American combat troops to the war in Vietnam, but according to Goldwater (his political opponent) and the Pentagon Papers (commissioned by his own secretary of defence), Johnson had already made up his mind to do just that.

Johnson has also been accused of lying to the public about the Gulf of Tonkin incident, the attack on American warships that precipitated American military intervention. According to Johnson, the USA had no role in provoking the North Vietnamese into attacking the USS *Maddox* – but not everyone agrees. Furthermore, the second attack – on the USS *C. Turner Joy* – may never have taken place.

The following evidence suggests that President Johnson provoked the Gulf of Tonkin incident and then used it as a pretext for going to war.

> Watch the Johnson campaign advertisement 'Daisy Girl' on YouTube: http://www.youtube.com/watch?v=9ld_r6pNsus.

> I repeat tonight that the United States was a provocateur in the Gulf of Tonkin episode. The United States was a part and parcel of the escalating of the war … As I said the other day, and repeat tonight, that has been the objective of Secretary McNamara for months and months, to escalate the war … We had American naval vessels in the vicinity. The Pentagon disputes how far away they were. There is no question that one of them was within the 12-mile limit of North Vietnam at the beginning of the bombardment. These are not among the facts that Americans were given in the President's television message, nor were they pointed out in the general news coverage of the *Maddox* incident. But they are the kind of facts that have been withheld so long that the American people do not know how we ever got started in the Vietnam War.
>
> Senator Wayne Morse, 21 August 1964

Insight

The Pentagon Papers showed that the Gulf of Tonkin incident was provoked by President Johnson to provide a pretext for military intervention. There were suspicions at the time that this was so. During the Senate debate on the Tonkin Gulf Resolution, several senators questioned the official version of events. As Senator George McGovern said, 'All of us have been puzzled, if not baffled, as to why a little state such as North Vietnam should seek a deliberate naval conflict with the United States.' Several key facts later emerged:

- North Vietnam claimed a 12-mile limit to its territorial waters. The United States recognised only a 10-mile limit. The USS *Maddox* was operating 11 miles off the coast of North Vietnam.
- The South Vietnamese navy was bombarding some North Vietnamese islands, and the USS *Maddox* was in close proximity to the South Vietnamese ships.
- The USS *C. Turner Joy*, which also reported itself under attack, later refused to confirm that an attack had taken place. A US pilot sent to search for the enemy ships found nothing in the area.

The Pentagon Papers later confirmed that the CIA was trying to provoke North Vietnam into launching a military strike that would justify American retaliation. Their main concern was that 'fear of escalation would probably restrain the communists' – in other words, the US Government *wanted* North Vietnam to attack the American ships.

The Pentagon Papers laid bare the entire history of US policy in Vietnam back to 1945. They revealed how successive governments:

- supported the French attempt to restore colonial control in Vietnam
- undermined the Geneva Accord of 1954
- created a country called South Vietnam in order to defend it
- supported the Government of Ngo Dinh Diem with $28 million of aid and military equipment
- played a key role in the 1963 coup d'etat that overthrew President Diem, though his murder came as an unpleasant surprise
- waged a war of covert operations against North Vietnam and communist forces in Laos
- deliberately and consistently misled the American public about US intentions.

These revelations were striking because they were concentrated in one document. Many of the facts from the 1940s and 1950s were probably public knowledge at the time, but no-one had ever put the story together. When viewed as a single narrative, the scale of America's interference in Vietnam became clear.

In today's world, revelations like the Pentagon Papers would probably come as no surprise. When Edward Snowden revealed secrets about the scale of NSA covert activities in 2013, many people just assumed that such activities were commonplace.

The Pentagon Papers, the Vietnam War and the Watergate Affair (see page 55) played a huge role in changing public attitudes. Before the 1960s most people were content to assume that their government could be trusted to tell the truth. People accepted that they did not know everything, and believed that what they did not know was kept from them for good reasons. All of this changed between 1965 and 1975. New phrases like 'being economical with the truth' and 'plausible deniability' entered the English language. The turning point came in the presidency of Richard Nixon. A political and social process that started with the assassination of President Kennedy transformed public awareness and gave rise to a new phenomenon: the conspiracy theory.

Counterfactual history and John F. Kennedy

Until 9/11 the most traumatic event in modern American history was the slaying of President Kennedy. Happening as it did in full public view, in the presence of his wife, the assassination of such a charismatic leader became the touchstone of a generation. It is true that everyone who lived through that moment remembered where they were and what they were doing when they heard the dreadful news. It happened on my

△ President John F. Kennedy moments before his assassination, Dallas, Texas, 22 November 1963.

mother's birthday, two days before my own, and for what it is worth the many conspiracy theories formed around the circumstances of his death have never persuaded me that the initial version of events was incorrect – that a lone gunman killed President Kennedy, for reasons that we will never know.

Conspiracy theories aside, the Kennedy assassination came to exert an extraordinary force on the interpretation of modern American history. It has been widely seen as a turning point, and invariably a turning point for the worse, where the natural order of events was corrupted, where history was steered down the wrong path. Many people have seen Kennedy's murder as the moment when everything began to go wrong. This is especially true for the Vietnam War.

Sadly, the most common way for people to become familiar with the Kennedy assassination is through the Oliver Stone film *JFK*. In this film Stone constructed a preposterous theory that Kennedy was the victim of a conspiracy so vast that it involved the Mafia, the CIA, the FBI, Vice President Johnson, the 'military-industrial complex', Fidel Castro of Cuba, and the Joint Chiefs of Staff. However, the central assumption made by the film – that America would have stayed out of the Vietnam War if Kennedy had survived – has been the subject of serious historical debate.

What would have happened in Vietnam if Kennedy had not been assassinated?

The theory that the Vietnam War was the tragic consequence of Kennedy's death began with some of the men who had served in Kennedy's Government. Chief among these was Robert McNamara, Kennedy's national security advisor, often regarded as the chief architect of the war. Along with other men like Arthur Schlesinger Jr, a historian whom Kennedy employed as a special assistant, McNamara believed that Kennedy would not have escalated the war as Johnson did. According to McNamara, in November 1963 Kennedy was planning to withdraw all 16,000 American advisers from Vietnam by 1965, starting with the 1,000 he actually did withdraw the month before he died. To begin with, most historians more or less dismissed such arguments, born out of feelings of grief for Kennedy and guilt for the war.

In recent years the theory that Kennedy might have withdrawn from Vietnam has gained a wider popularity. Assuming that he won the 1964 election, the argument goes that Kennedy would then have been free to dispose of Vietnam without fear of the public reaction, if he judged it a lost cause. The Bay of Pigs fiasco and the Cuban Missile Crisis left Kennedy with profound misgivings about the advice coming to him from over-confident military officers. We have already seen (page 31–32) that Kennedy refused Walt Rostow's advice to begin a major bombing campaign of North Vietnam. Various historians have taken up the theme, including David Kaiser in *American Tragedy*, who argued that Kennedy was 'the most sceptical senior official' about Vietnam in his own Government, exercising caution where others urged action.

By contrast, the dominant view for many years was that Kennedy's actions indicated a deepening commitment to South Vietnam that could only have ended in war. How could the man who committed 16,000 advisers to Vietnam walk away from the conflict? Given the fact that Johnson kept the Kennedy foreign policy team intact after 1964, this view stressed the continuity between Kennedy and Johnson. On the day Kennedy was assassinated, he was on his way to make a speech in which he would have reaffirmed America's role as guardian of the free world, including the 'painful, risky and costly' commitment to South Vietnam. Rostow was adamant that Kennedy would have followed the same path as Johnson. As a Democrat, Kennedy needed to balance his liberal domestic reforms with the rhetoric of a Cold War warrior.

It therefore appears that the arguments between 'orthodox' and 'revisionist' historians have been strangely inverted in the case of Kennedy counter-factualism. Generally speaking, the 'orthodox' position is the one that views Vietnam as an unwinnable mistake. 'Revisionist' historians, by contrast, are those that have argued that Vietnam was a just war in a good cause, thrown away by mismanagement. Where Kennedy's death is concerned, though, the roles are reversed: the 'revisionists' are those who mourn the lost opportunity to avoid the conflict, while the 'orthodox' historians stress the continuity of American policy and Kennedy's role in digging the hole into which America fell. Perhaps this inversion of historical perspectives is what E.P. Thompson was referring to when he described counterfactual history as 'unhistorical shit'.

Since President Truman (1945–52) American presidents have only been allowed to serve two four-year terms in office.

5 Why did it take so long for the USA to get out of Vietnam?

In 1966 Simon and Garfunkel released their third album, *Scarborough Fair*, a record bought by millions. The final track, *Seven O'Clock News/ Silent Night*, contained in the background the recording of a radio news broadcast for 3 August 1966. Audible against the Christmas carol was the following news item:

Former Vice President Richard Nixon says that unless there is a substantial increase in the present war effort in Vietnam, the USA should look forward to five more years of war. In a speech before the Convention of the Veterans of Foreign Wars in New York, Nixon also said opposition to the war in this country is the greatest single weapon working against the US.

Three years later Nixon was president of the United States, elected on the promise that he had a secret plan to end the war in Vietnam. Yet the war carried on for another four years in which a further 22,000 Americans died. This final four-year period was a significant length of time when compared with America's experience of other wars – three years in Korea, three and a half years in the Second World War and 18 months in the First World War. Why did it take so long to get out of Vietnam?

Timeline of key events in the ending of the Vietnam War

Date	Events
31 March 1968	President Johnson halts the bombing of North Vietnam and announces peace initiatives to end the war
November 1968	Paris peace talks begin Richard Nixon advises President Thieu of South Vietnam not to negotiate until after the American presidential election Richard Nixon elected president
January 1969	President Nixon orders a thorough review of Vietnam policy
March 1969	USA begins bombing the Ho Chi Minh Trail and North Vietnamese bases in Cambodia in an operation called the MENU series of attacks
May 1969	Battle of Hamburger Hill – the last major battle of General Westmoreland's strategy of attrition
June 1969	American troop reductions begin – first step of 'Vietnamisation' Nixon meets President Thieu on Midway Island in the Pacific

Date	Events
3 November 1969	Nixon's 'Silent Majority' speech, in which he claims that most Americans support the war effort
March 1970	Cambodia – pro-American General Lon Nol overthrows Prince Sihanouk, leading North Vietnam to support the radical communist Khmer Rouge
29 April – 30 June 1970	Combined ARVN–American incursion into Cambodia
4 May 1970	Four antiwar protestors shot dead at Kent State University, Ohio, by National Guard troops
9 May 1970	Nixon encounters antiwar protestors at the Lincoln Memorial
February 1971	ARVN invasion into Laos in attempt to cut the Ho Chi Minh Trail ends in disaster for the South Vietnamese
March 1971	'Linebacker 1' – Nixon begins heavy bombing of North Vietnam
February 1972	Nixon's visit to China
March 1972	Communist Easter Offensive begins
May 1972	Nixon's visit to the Soviet Union – signs **ABM Treaty** and **SALT 1**
October 1972	Communist and American negotiators in Paris reach agreement in talks that do not include South Vietnam
November 1972	President Nixon re-elected
December 1972	'Linebacker 2' – further heavy bombing of North Vietnam
January 1973	Paris Peace Accords signed

What were the two sides looking for?

One reason it took so long to make peace is because, at the beginning of the peace process, the Americans and the North Vietnamese were so far apart in their demands. Before a deal could be struck there had to be movement on both sides.

North Vietnam's demands
- Thieu regime to be removed in South Vietnam
- NLF to take at least partial power in Saigon
- An 'in-place' ceasefire, leaving communist forces in control of areas they held in South Vietnam

The United States' demands
- Thieu Government to remain in power
- Complete mutual withdrawal of US and communist forces from South Vietnam

ABM Treaty
Anti-Ballistic Missile Treaty, a treaty with the Soviet Union that limited each country to a single defensive system against enemy nuclear missiles, thus preserving MAD (Mutual Assured Destruction), the keystone of nuclear deterrence.

SALT 1
Strategic Arms Limitations Treaty no. 1, a treaty with the Soviet Union that imposed a freeze on the development of new nuclear weapons. This was the first major step towards slowing down the nuclear arms race.

Enquiry Focus: Why did it take so long for the USA to get out of Vietnam?

The introduction to this chapter may have given you the impression that American actions alone were responsible for prolonging the Vietnam War. However, we also need to examine the roles of several other countries (shown in the diagram below) in order to build up an effective answer to this question.

Your task in this chapter is to collect evidence showing how the actions and decisions of each country helped to delay the end of the war.

1 After reading each section of text, make detailed notes using the points on the diagram as a guide. These notes should explain how the actions and decisions of each country contributed to the prolonging of the war.

2 After taking your notes, summarise the key points on your copy of the diagram below.

Do not assume that each section of text relates to just one country. For example, there is no single section on the roles of either Russia or China. Most sections provide information about several countries.

At the end of the chapter you will then use this evidence to construct an overall answer to the question.

North Vietnam
- determination to achieve an outright victory over South Vietnam
- inability to achieve outright victory over American forces
- aid from USSR and China

Soviet Union
- desire to maintain prestige as the only communist superpower
- determination to support North Vietnam
- timing of Nixon's visit to Moscow

China
- concern that war might spread into Laos and Cambodia
- determination to support North Vietnam
- timing of Nixon's visit to China

United States
- 'peace with honour'/American credibility
- Nixon's grand strategy
- impact of elections
- impact of antiwar movement

Reasons delaying the end of the war

South Vietnam
- President Thieu's personal ambition
- strength of ARVN forces

Nixon's strategy for ending the Vietnam War

In 1969 the Republicans took power and so there were many changes in the key personnel running American foreign policy. These changes are summarised in the illustration below. They had important consequences for the way the war was fought.

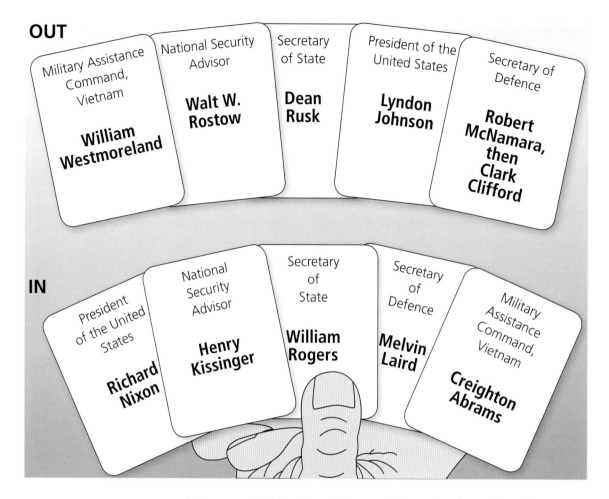

OUT

Military Assistance Command, Vietnam

William Westmoreland

National Security Advisor

Walt W. Rostow

Secretary of State

Dean Rusk

President of the United States

Lyndon Johnson

Secretary of Defence

Robert McNamara, then Clark Clifford

IN

President of the United States

Richard Nixon

National Security Advisor

Henry Kissinger

Secretary of State

William Rogers

Secretary of Defence

Melvin Laird

Military Assistance Command, Vietnam

Creighton Abrams

In January 1969 President Nixon and his national security advisor, Henry Kissinger, began developing a grand strategy for ending the war. Their main concern was that America should get out of Vietnam without losing international credibility – 'peace with honour', as Nixon called it. While Nixon spoke publicly of 'a lasting peace in the world', in private Kissinger was assuring the Chinese that all America was looking for was 'a decent interval' – perhaps two or three years – between an American withdrawal and the collapse of South Vietnam. This ruled out any cut-and-run strategy involving a precipitate American withdrawal that would leave South Vietnam exposed to sudden defeat. In his Address to the Nation on the War in Vietnam of 3 November 1969 Nixon explained that he could not simply blame the Democrats for the war and pull out. As a result, finding an acceptable way to end the war would be long and difficult.

By this stage American credibility had replaced the domino theory as the overriding American concern in Vietnam. The US Government was now less worried about the spread of communism in Southeast Asia than it was about the global impact of America abandoning an ally. Nixon's strategy required simultaneous efforts in several areas:

1   **Applying more pressure on North Vietnam**. Nixon intensified the bombing of North Vietnam and the Ho Chi Minh Trail, using America's strategic bomber force of B-52s. The MENU series of attacks targeted Cambodia, while Linebackers 1 and 2 focused on North Vietnam. Nixon gave the US Air Force greater control of the choice of targets.

2   **Splitting the communist bloc by improving relations with China and with the Soviet Union**. Nixon hoped to encourage Russia and China to compete for American friendship, leading to a thaw in the Cold War that would lead to progress in arms limitations talks and greater understanding of each other's vital interests. Détente with the communist great powers might also exert pressure on North Vietnam to come to terms.

3   **Vietnamisation**. A slow, phased withdrawal of American ground forces, accompanied by intense American air support for the ARVN and training and logistical support for ARVN forces. Vietnamisation would help to undermine the American antiwar movement and improve Nixon's relations with Congress.

4   **Paris peace talks with North Vietnam**. Formal peace talks helped give the impression that progress was being made towards ending the war. The real diplomacy with North Vietnam, however, was carried out privately between Henry Kissinger and Le Due Tho, the North Vietnamese representative. This enabled Kissinger to gradually exclude President Thieu of South Vietnam, an insuperable obstacle to an agreement.

Nixon's strategy took time to work. Relations between Russia, China and North Vietnam were complex. North Vietnam was intransigent: the failure of the ARVN incursion into Laos in 1971 revealed the weakness of Vietnamisation, and North Vietnam wanted to assert its independence from Soviet or Chinese control. Russia was keen to reach an agreement with America but also wanted to retain its historic leadership of international communism over China. China was worried that the Soviet Union, in league with North Vietnam, might increase its power in Cambodia at China's expense – in other words, China itself was coming to fear a 'domino effect' in Southeast Asia. The success of Nixon's strategy therefore depended on a coming together of various developments – the diplomatic and military planets had to come into alignment before his grand strategy could work.

The war intensifies

As we have seen, Nixon's strategy required America to apply more pressure on North Vietnam by removing some of the constraints that had stayed Johnson's hand before 1968. The invasions of Cambodia (1970) and Laos (1971) were part of this development. Johnson's rules of engagement had prevented any violation of international borders, at least by ordinary combat troops. Nixon was not so particular, though the fear of domestic reactions limited the time and extent of what he could do. The incursion into Cambodia only lasted two months, and the incursion into Laos was carried out by ARVN forces. However, when communist forces threatened the flanks of the ARVN retreat, the South Vietnamese Army was saved by massive and repeated American air strikes.

The bombing of North Vietnam in the 'Linebacker' series was qualitatively different from Johnson's 'Rolling Thunder' campaign. There was less political interference in the selection of targets, as shown by the decision to mine the harbour at Haiphong despite the presence of numerous Soviet ships. There is evidence to show that Nixon's bombing campaigns had an impact on North Vietnamese decisions: for example, the Christmas bombing of 1972 forced North Vietnam's leaders to question the wisdom of holding out for better terms, helping to achieve a breakthrough in the Paris peace negotiations in January 1973. Even then, however, Nixon had to observe some political constraints: plans to destroy North Vietnam's extensive dyke system were abandoned for fear of further antiwar protests in the United States.

◁ Half the American strategic bomber force – 212 B-52 bombers from America's Strategic Air Command – delivered the MENU series of air strikes, plus the Linebacker 1 and Linebacker 2 campaigns against North Vietnam. The bombers flew in box formations of three planes, as shown, dropping their bombs in unison to produce 'Arc Light' strikes that destroyed everything in a rectangular square mile.

The impact of domestic politics

One persistent criticism made of American foreign policy is that it is a hostage to American politics, especially American elections. What is the evidence, if any, that Nixon's strategy to end the Vietnam War was influenced by his desire to win presidential elections?

In the autumn of 1968 Richard Nixon feared that President Johnson was about to deliver a peace agreement with North Vietnam that would hand the keys of the White House to Nixon's Democratic rival, Hubert Humphrey. Using a '**back channel**' (Anna Chennault, a Chinese-American Republican), Nixon advised Thieu to reject peace talks before the November election, with the promise that Thieu would get a better deal from the Republicans than he would from the Democrats. Nixon therefore colluded with a foreign leader to foil the public policy of the US Government.

Some Americans – myself included – believed at the time that Nixon would draw out the war in such a way as to encourage the American people to re-elect him in 1972. This is a difficult idea to grasp – surely if Nixon delayed ending the war, then the American people would blame him for this and vote for his Democratic rival? Not necessarily; he might be able to claim that peace negotiations had reached a critical point where only he could reach agreement with North Vietnam. The 1972 presidential election certainly exerted some control over the peace process: it set the timetable for Vietnamisation, forcing Nixon to withdraw most American troops within four years. By mid-1972 American troop levels had fallen to under 50,000. As it happened, the Paris Peace Accords were signed on 27 January 1973, just one week after Nixon's reinauguration. Given the complexities of the peace-making process, it is probably going too far to suggest that President Nixon played politics with the lives of American soldiers. However, the Watergate Affair revealed Nixon's paranoia about re-election, and the lengths to which his administration would go to ensure that he won in 1972.

Back channel
An unofficial diplomatic route – perhaps a private contact, or an unofficial intermediary.

Nixon, Kissinger and the 'madman' theory

The USA's plans to destroy the irrigation dykes in North Vietnam were part of a threatened campaign of all-out warfare that began to call Nixon's sanity into question. Nixon informed Republican senators that he was considering an invasion of North Vietnam; he also considered the use of **tactical nuclear weapons**. Kissinger let the Soviet Union know that Nixon was capable of making irrational decisions, raising the prospect of an American president pushed beyond the limits of reason – the 'madman' theory. What could happen if the President of the United States went nuts? What if Nixon no longer cared whether the war spread into Laos and Cambodia, or if China got involved?

Tactical nuclear weapons
Relatively small 'battlefield' nuclear weapons fired from artillery.

Kissinger knew that Nixon was behaving strangely. He was drinking heavily. He repeatedly watched the war film *Patton: Lust for Glory*, and listened to the Richard Rodgers recording of **Victory At Sea** at full volume. Early on the morning of 9 May 1970, just five days after the Kent State shootings, Nixon walked out of the White House with minimal security and made his way over to the Lincoln Memorial to talk to antiwar demonstrators. According to eyewitnesses, Nixon was rambling about football and other inconsequential matters, as if he was just another politician. The leader of the free world could not take such risks. Kissinger was genuinely concerned about Nixon's mental state, but he also saw an opportunity to use it as a diplomatic weapon. Maybe the Russians could be frightened into forcing North Vietnam to accept America's terms.

Victory at Sea
The soundtrack to a popular American TV series about the role played by Allied naval power in defeating Japan and Nazi Germany in the Second World War.

Ultimately, the 'madman' theory failed to have much impact on the communist powers. They saw through the bluff and refused to be panicked into a quick settlement. Ironically, as the war came to an end and the Watergate Affair began to consume his presidency, Nixon genuinely did begin to show signs of irrational paranoia. By the time he left office in 1974, people were glad that he was relinquishing control over the launch codes for America's nuclear arsenal.

The impact of the antiwar movement in America on the duration of the war

Both orthodox and revisionist historians have claimed, for different reasons, that antiwar protests forced America to withdraw from the Vietnam War. The orthodox view gives the protest movement credit for forcing Nixon to speed up the process of Vietnamisation, thus hastening the end of the war. In contrast, revisionists blame the protest movement for forcing America to abandon prematurely a war it could have won, and for preventing Nixon from fighting the war even more vigorously. In recent years, however, historians have begun to focus more precisely on the impact of public protests on the decision-makers responsible for American policy. John Dumbrell, in *Rethinking the Vietnam War* (2012), argued that the antiwar movement was a qualified success because it influenced the decisions Presidents Johnson and Nixon felt able to make. For example, Nixon's decision to move faster towards Vietnamisation after 1970 was driven by the threat of a 'spring offensive' by the protesters. By the 1970s many of the soldiers sent to Vietnam had themselves taken part in antiwar protests. However, he argued, there is no proof that declining public

△ Antiwar protestors produced this version of the famous Uncle Sam recruiting poster in 1969.

support for the war was the result of the protest movement. Both Johnson and Nixon despised the protesters and used the demonstrations to rally support from what Nixon called the 'Silent Majority', supported by press coverage that was mostly hostile to the demonstrators. As we have seen, in 1966 Nixon referred to opposition to the war as 'the greatest single factor working against the US' – far from hastening the end of the war, he believed that antiwar protests in America delayed the war's end. Nixon believed the protests made it impossible for America to fight with full force, and encouraged the enemy to aim for an outright victory instead of negotiating an end to the fighting.

It is possible, however, that the antiwar movement in America had a negligible impact on how long the war lasted. As Vietnamisation progressed, the size and frequency of antiwar demonstrations declined, to the point where the US Government no longer needed to take them into account in peace negotiations. In addition, President Nixon actually turned the protests on the protestors, marginalising the movement and portraying it as anti-American. His 'Silent Majority' speech in 1969 seems to have struck a chord, reminding the nation that the vast majority of Americans did not take to the streets in protest. In 1970 there were so-called 'hard hat' protests by demonstrators supporting the war – the 'hard hats' represented their determination to see the war through to the end. The counter-argument to this is, of course, that Vietnamisation was itself forced on Nixon by antiwar protests.

Dealing with South Vietnam

One of the factors holding up a peace agreement was the Vietnamese themselves – both in the South and the North. During the 1960s and early 1970s a policy known as détente had been developing, gradually improving America's relationships with Russia and China. As détente came together in the spring of 1972, the main obstacle to peace was no longer superpower Cold War rivalry, but the chief protagonists in the war – North and South Vietnam. To a certain extent, they held the **superpowers** hostage. For example, America might want to strike a deal with China and the Soviet Union over the future of Vietnam, but what if President Thieu of South Vietnam refused the terms? The superpowers had to bring their clients to heel.

In 1969 President Nixon signalled a major shift in American Cold War strategy – the 'Nixon Doctrine'. America, he said, would stand by its treaty commitments, but it would no longer fight wars on behalf of its Asian allies. If countries in Southeast Asia were to repel the advance of communism, they would have to do it with their own troops. There would be no more Vietnams. This put pressure on President Thieu because it implied that America was running out of patience with South Vietnam.

Superpower
Strictly speaking, the only superpowers in the world were the USA and the Soviet Union. Communist China was a great regional power but did not have the necessary nuclear weaponry, naval power, economic strength or world influence to qualify as a superpower.

To drive the point home, Nixon had a meeting with President Thieu on Midway Island, in the Pacific Ocean. Nixon spelled out to Thieu that the period of American escalation was over. Vietnamisation was the new policy. American troop withdrawals would begin immediately. The gradual withdrawal of American forces put pressure on Thieu to agree to the terms America would negotiate with the communists, but he knew that the United States could not withdraw all of its forces without a negotiated peace. President Thieu's policy was to hold out for better terms – just as Nixon had advised him to do in 1968. One of these terms was that Thieu himself would remain in power in South Vietnam, a demand he knew was unacceptable to the communists.

By July 1972 secret negotiations between America and North Vietnam were close to success. North Vietnam dropped its insistence that President Thieu be removed immediately from power. The Americans accepted that prisoners of war (PoWs) would not be exchanged until after a settlement was agreed. Kissinger also conceded that no American forces would be left in South Vietnam after the war, as they were in South Korea. But President Thieu saw this as an American betrayal and refused to accept it.

Ultimately, the United States was prepared to abandon South Vietnam to its fate, provided that a decent period of time elapsed between the American withdrawal and the final communist offensive. In order to get Thieu's agreement, some further concessions had to be wrung from the North Vietnamese. This was achieved by the Linebacker 2 bombing of Christmas 1972.

Dealing with North Vietnam

In March 1972, four years after the failure of the Tet Offensive, North Vietnam and the NLF launched a new general assault on South Vietnam – the Easter Offensive. By this stage Vietnamisation was well advanced, and it fell to ARVN troops, supported by intensive American bombing, to hold back the communist attacks. The Easter Offensive was an attempt to move the war into the decisive final stage, in which guerrilla warfare gave way to large-scale conventional attacks by the North Vietnamese Army (see Phase 3, page 27). It turned out to

be premature: in the Central Highlands the NVA attack on Kontum was halted with devastating loss of life by American 'Arc Light' strikes, delivered on massed NVA infantry caught in the open. Nevertheless, as the map shows, many parts of South Vietnam were now under communist control.

Why did North Vietnam choose this moment to launch an offensive? The NVA was now well equipped with heavy weaponry, including tanks and artillery, imported from China and the Soviet Union. American troop levels were down to 95,000 men, with further reductions already announced. North Vietnam also wanted to show that it still had the initiative because the new American strategy of counter-insurgency, Vietnamisation and increased air strikes seemed to be achieving some success.

Most importantly, however, the North Vietnamese wanted to win the war before China and the Soviet Union forced them to accept an

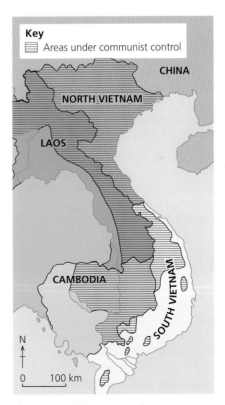

△ A map of Indochina showing areas under firm communist control at the time of the Paris Peace Accord, January 1973.

armistice that left US forces in South Vietnam. Until 1972 the communist great powers had encouraged North Vietnam to fight for an all-out victory against the Americans. It suited the Soviet Union for America to be tied down in a war it could neither win nor lose. China was hoping that North Vietnam would be able to achieve an outright military victory. Between them, their support strengthened the hardliners in Hanoi, which in turn hardened North Vietnam's position in the Paris negotiations.

By Easter 1972, however, the Soviet and Chinese positions had begun to shift. Brezhnev, the Soviet premier, was hinting to America that if the Americans withdrew their troops, the USSR would encourage North Vietnam to allow a decent interval to elapse before conquering the South. However, North Vietnam was not prepared to accept this until it was once again on the receiving end of American air power which smashed the Easter Offensive and threatened to completely destroy North Vietnam's economic infrastructure. By January 1973 North Vietnam was ready to accept America's terms.

Peace with honour?

In January 1973 America, North and South Vietnam and the NLF signed the Paris Peace Accords that ended American involvement in the Vietnam War. The terms were as follows:

- an 'in-place' ceasefire that left communist forces in possession of large parts of South Vietnam
- the withdrawal of American forces to begin immediately and to be completed within 60 days
- prisoners of war on both sides to be released and the remains of dead soldiers to be repatriated
- negotiations to begin between the Government of South Vietnam and the NLF that would allow the people of South Vietnam to decide their future through free elections
- Vietnam to be reunited 'step by step and through peaceful means'.

It is clear from these terms that North Vietnam had won the war. The only significant concession won by the Americans was that North Vietnam dropped its insistence on the immediate removal of President Thieu and the inclusion of NLF personnel in the Government of South Vietnam. The release of American POWs was of major importance to American public opinion, but this was not one of America's original war aims – if there had been no war, there would have been no prisoners. In effect, the terms of the treaty were not very different from those that could have been negotiated in 1965, before the deaths of 56,000 Americans.

'But we are professionals: we have to go on fighting till the politicians tell us to stop. Probably they will get together and agree to the same peace that we could have had at the beginning, making nonsense of all these years.'

From Graham Greene, *The Quiet American* (1955), a novel about American involvement in the French phase of the war in Vietnam.

The end

On 30 April 1975 an extraordinary scene unfolded in the South China Sea. South Vietnamese pilots were flying their Huey helicopters out to an American aircraft carrier and landing on the ship. When the crews abandoned their Hueys, the Americans tipped the helicopters over the side to make way for more to land. Some pilots were ditching their helicopters in the sea.

A few days before this, an argument over a tree broke out in the American Embassy in Saigon, the capital of South Vietnam. The American ambassador refused to accept that South Vietnam was falling to the communists. His advisers were telling him the war was lost, that it was time to get out. In order to evacuate the embassy staff and hundreds of South Vietnamese, they needed to cut down a tree in the embassy grounds so that the helicopters could land. The ambassador refused: the tree was a symbol of America's commitment to its ally, and he would not budge. But finally, with North Vietnamese tanks in the outskirts of Saigon and hundreds of South Vietnamese desperately besieging the embassy for evacuation, he gave in. The tree came down.

It was too late to get everybody out. The South Vietnamese in the embassy grounds were people who had worked for the Americans. Their lives were in danger if the communists caught them. But in the end, the Americans had to choose who to save and who to leave behind. On 30 April it came down to nationality: the US Marines quietly spirited the Americans up the stairs to the embassy roof and bolted the doors, leaving the Vietnamese on the ground floor. America had abandoned its ally.

The defeat of South Vietnam actually came as a relief for many Americans. For a long time, most people thought it was inevitable. For nine years American soldiers had fought for what seemed to be a hopeless cause. Now the curtain was coming down on a war that everyone wanted to forget.

▷ South Vietnamese helicopters being thrown overboard from an American aircraft carrier on 30 April 1975. This scene marks the lowest point for American prestige in the twentieth century.

■ Concluding your enquiry

The diagram you have been completing should now show the main reasons why each country's attitudes and decisions delayed the signing of a peace agreement. You can use the completed diagram to help you to construct an answer to the enquiry: why did it take so long for the USA to get out of Vietnam? However, before you write this essay, think about and discuss the following questions:

1 Which factors (not countries) played the greatest part in prolonging the war? Think about what the different countries may have had in common in attitudes and fears. For example, both America and China were concerned (for different reasons) that the war might spread to Laos and Cambodia.

2 Here are four statements that attempt to answer our enquiry question. What evidence would you use to support and challenge each of them?

 a) President Thieu's determination to remain in power did most to prolong the war.

 b) America's desire for 'peace with honour' did most to prolong the war.

 c) Soviet and Chinese fear of US power did most to prolong the war.

 d) North Vietnam's determination to win the war outright did most to prolong the war.

3 Now plan and write your essay.

What changed to enable peace to be made in 1973?

So far this chapter has focused on why it took so long for the war to be brought to an end. However, there is another, strongly linked question that we do not have time to cover in detail but is well worth considering. This is, what changed to enable peace to be made in 1973?

■ Enquiry Focus

You can use a diagram to record the reasons why peace was finally achieved.

Record on your diagram the *things that changed* to allow peace to be made. The example of North Vietnam has been completed for you.

To obtain the information that you need:

> **North Vietnam**
> - pressure from the USSR to reach an agreement with the USA, on the understanding that it would be OK to defeat South Vietnam once a decent interval of time had passed
> - pressure from China to reach an agreement with the USA, for fear that North Vietnam would spread Soviet influence into Cambodia
> - Linebacker 2 bombing by the Americans helped defeat the hardliners in North Vietnam who were holding out for an outright victory

South Vietnam		Soviet Union
	Reasons peace was finally achieved	
United States		China

1 read the text on détente (below)
2 re-read the earlier part of this chapter, this time identifying the changes that took place that led to peace.

Once you have done this for all five countries, then you should be ready to write an essay to answer this question: what changed to enable peace to be made in Vietnam in 1973?

Détente

The process of 'détente' began after the Cuban Missile Crisis (1962), when Russia and America came to the brink of nuclear war. The crisis frightened Kennedy and Khrushchev so much that they began looking for ways to defuse the tensions between the USA and the Soviet Union. During the 1960s various steps were taken:

- ■ a telephone hotline was set up to enable the Soviet and American leaders to communicate directly in any future crisis

- ■ an atmospheric test-ban treaty banned nuclear tests above ground

- ■ a non-proliferation treaty tried to prevent any more countries from obtaining nuclear weapons.

Khrushchev was overthrown in 1964 (probably because of the Cuban Missile crisis), but his successor Leonid Brezhnev continued the process of trying to improve relations with America. In fact, the Vietnam War showed that a form of détente was already at work, since the Russians backed away from any direct confrontation with the Americans.

As president, Nixon wanted to develop détente to the point where the great powers recognised each other's special interests and spheres of influence, in order to avoid mistakes like those which led to the Cuban Missile Crisis. He knew that each country had reasons for adopting less confrontational policies. The Soviet Union needed American grain and wanted to slow down the nuclear arms race with the United States. Communist China wanted official recognition and a seat at the United Nations (UN), which was currently occupied by Taiwan. Nixon also saw an opportunity to drive a wedge between China and the Soviet Union. Soviet and Chinese soldiers had fought a seven-month undeclared war during a border dispute in 1969. China resented the USSR's claim to lead the communist world and, as we have seen (page 83), China feared that a North Vietnamese victory would result in the expansion of Soviet influence into Cambodia and Laos.

However, as long as America was fighting for victory in Vietnam, it was impossible to split the communist bloc. Détente would only work when it was clear that the USA accepted that a military victory in Vietnam was impossible (which was clear by 1972). Therefore détente depended on getting out of Vietnam. The reverse was also true: once the Cold War myth was shattered (namely that communism was simply a global conspiracy orchestrated by Moscow), the survival of South Vietnam would no longer be important to the USA. As long as a decent interval elapsed between the final American withdrawal and the collapse of South Vietnam, the Americans could claim to have saved their honour and credibility.

▽ Détente: power relationships between the USA, the USSR and China in 1972.

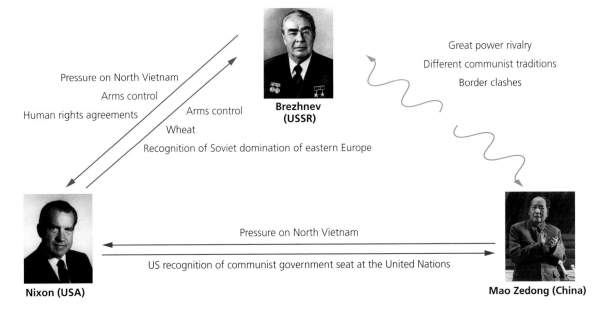

Pressure on North Vietnam
Arms control
Human rights agreements

Arms control
Wheat
Recognition of Soviet domination of eastern Europe

Brezhnev (USSR)

Great power rivalry
Different communist traditions
Border clashes

Pressure on North Vietnam
US recognition of communist government seat at the United Nations

Nixon (USA)

Mao Zedong (China)

6 How is the Vietnam War remembered?

■ **Enquiry Focus:** The academic debate: Why do historians disagree about the Vietnam War?

1 On pages 12–13 you were introduced to the debates about the Vietnam War, with a short focus on orthodox and revisionist views. Before proceeding go back to this short section and read it again.

2 You were also encouraged to make notes on these debates whenever you saw the following symbol ✗, filing your notes under 'orthodox' and 'revisionist' columns wherever possible. Make certain that your set of notes is complete. To assist you, here is a table to fill in. The first two issues, taken from page 13, have been done for you:

Orthodox interpretation	Issues	Revisionist interpretation
The war was based on a false view of monolithic world communism and therefore not necessary.	Was the war necessary?	The monolithic view of world communism was correct, so the war needed to be fought.
America got sucked into an unwinnable quagmire.	Could America have won the war?	America could have won the war if American politicians had allowed the US military a free hand.
	Was America shackled to a corpse? (pages 22–25)	
	Did President Johnson undermine the effectiveness of the bombing of North Vietnam? (pages 32–33)	

You may expand on this table to answer other questions, using an orthodox and revisionist interpretation: Did General Westmoreland lose the war through his policy of attrition? (pages 34–35); Could General Abrams' 'One War' strategy have succeeded if it had been given more time? (pages 36–37); Did the Vietnam War contribute to America's economic problems? (pages 48–49); Was the Vietnam War illegal under the American Constitution? (page 75); What would have happened in Vietnam if President Kennedy had not been assassinated? (pages 77–78); Did domestic politics in the USA prolong the Vietnam War? (pages 84–86), and; Did the antiwar movement in America shorten the war? (page 85).

Before continuing, you need to be clear what is meant by, 'orthodox' and 'revisionist' interpretations.

The phrase **orthodox interpretation** describes the dominant historical view that emerged from the war and dominated historical writing about Vietnam from the 1960s until at least the 1980s. This viewpoint regarded Vietnam as a war that America a) should not have fought and b) could not have won. This does not mean that everyone at that time agreed with this view, nor does it mean that this view has been replaced by revisionism. It does mean, however, that any historian challenging these two assumptions faced an uphill struggle to gain acceptance.

The phrase **revisionist interpretation** describes books and articles that have challenged the orthodox interpretation. Most revisionists believe that Vietnam was a war that America should have fought and could have won. Indeed, some argue that America *did* win the Vietnam War, in that it achieved its main objective of preventing the spread of communism in Southeast Asia. This definition does not mean that most historians now agree with this view.

How useful are these labels for students trying to understand the historiography of the Vietnam War? Some arguments do not fit neatly into either orthodox or revisionist viewpoints, but for students setting out on the road to understanding Vietnam historiography, these labels may serve a useful purpose. They draw attention to the fact that history is a debate that changes constantly in response to new research, contemporary events and the beliefs and opinions of the historians themselves. In the case of Vietnam, some of these factors can best be understood visually, as the following diagram shows.

Journalists who covered the war whose opinions came to dominate thinking about Vietnam during and shortly after the defeat, forming the orthodox views that the war was misguided and unwinnable.
For example:
- David Halberstam, *The Making of a Quagmire* (1965) and *The Best and Brightest* (1972). The latter book especially formed the bedrock of the orthodox view for its criticism of the over-confidence of Kennedy and Johnson's foreign policy advisers.
- Neil Sheehan, *A Bright Shining Lie* (1988), criticised the US Government for failing to heed warnings about the weaknesses of the South Vietnamese regime.

US officers who served in Vietnam published books blaming America's politicians for the defeat.
Their basic premise was that political interference prevented the US military from carrying out its mission. For example:
- Admiral U.S.G. Sharp, *Strategy For Defeat: Vietnam in Retrospect* (1978). Sharp argued that the gradualism of Rolling Thunder enabled North Vietnam to create formidable air defences and created the impression that America was heavily influenced by domestic antiwar opinion.
- Harry Summers, *On Strategy: A Critical Analysis of the Vietnam War* (1982). Summers argued that American leaders failed to grasp the elementary principles of warfare outlined by the Napoleonic strategist Carl von Clausewitz in *On War*, required reading at the US Military Academy at West Point.
However, other historians continue to put the orthodox interpretation, for example:
- Mark Clodfelter, *The Limits of Air Power: The American Bombing of North Vietnam* (1989). Clodfelter argued that air power alone cannot win wars, a point illustrated not only in Vietnam but also in the Second World War.

Original arguments reflecting the debates within the Johnson and Nixon administrations continued to generate new publications.
Most famously:
- Robert McNamara, *Argument Without End* (1994) and, especially, *In Retrospect* (1995). McNamara, the 'chief architect' of the war, apologised for the mistakes he and others had made in the 1960s, in the hope that future decision-makers would avoid making similar errors.
- W. W. Rostow, *Case for the War* (1995), was an angry response to McNamara. Rostow argued that Vietnam was a necessary war that had succeeded in limiting communist ambitions in Southeast Asia, and that America's only mistake was that it failed to fight the war vigorously enough – surprising, perhaps, given that the gradualism of Rolling Thunder was his idea.

Why do historians disagree about aspects of the Vietnam War?

New research reveals new facts and insights into different aspects of the war.
In recent years the emphasis of historical research has started to shift away from the Americans towards other participants, particularly North Vietnam and South Vietnam. For example:
- L.-H.T. Nguyen, *Hanoi's War: An International History of the War for Peace in Vietnam* (2012). Nguyen provided a North Vietnamese perspective, broadening the international dimension by showing how North Vietnam exploited Chinese–Russian competition for leadership of the war.
- J.M. Chapman, *Cauldron of Resistance: Ngo Dinh Diem, the United States, and 1950s Southern Vietnam* (2013). Chapman explored the conflicts between Ngo Dinh Diem's regime and the so-called 'religious sects' in the 1950s, shedding new light on the Vietnamese context of the political crisis that eventually led to American intervention.
Research also continues to shed new light on the American war. For example:
- Dr David Milne, *America's Rasputin: Walt Rostow and the Vietnam War* (2008). Milne described how Walt Rostow developed a historical theory of the 'take-off' of industrialisation and applied it to Vietnam, influencing President Johnson's conduct of the war until 1968.

Contemporary events.
As time moves on, the impact of current affairs has a powerful effect on historical interpretations. It enables us to see the past in greater perspective, but contemporary issues can also drag historical arguments into the present day. This is such an important influence on Vietnam historiography that a separate enquiry task has been created for it below.

Neoconservative revisionism linked to current American politics.
As mentioned in Chapter 3, since the 1960s there has been a marked shift to the right in American politics. This has had a powerful impact on American thinking about the Vietnam War. The most important examples of this argued that, at different times, America was actually winning the Vietnam War:
- Lewis Sorley, *A Better War: The Unexamined Victories and Final Tragedy of America's Last Years in Vietnam* (1999). Sorley argued that in 1972, as American troops were pulling out, South Vietnam was actually winning the war with the support of American air power. But when Congress passed the War Powers Resolution and withdrew financial support for the war, it doomed South Vietnam to defeat.
- Mark Moyar, *Triumph Forsaken* (2006). Moyar's argument is that Ngo Dinh Diem was getting the communist insurgency under control when the Kennedy administration lost patience with the slow pace of reform in South Vietnam and colluded with the military coup that led to Diem's death. This in turn undermined the effectiveness of the ARVN forces in the critical period when President Johnson decided to commit troops.

Neoconservativism
An American political movement that regards liberal politics as a failure and stresses the promotion of democracy, if necessary by military force. Neoconservative thinking lay behind the invasion of Iraq in 2003, aiming to bring democracy and stability to the Middle East.

■ The impact of contemporary events on Vietnam historiography

On your own copy of the table below, place the titles and dates of the histories mentioned above with a short (one-sentence) summary of their main point. Where books were published earlier or later in a decade, try to indicate this in the table by placing it to the top or bottom of the appropriate column. Several entries have been done for you, including two books not mentioned in the text.

Events

2000s

The century began with 9/11, the most serious terrorist attack of modern times. This led the USA to fight two major wars:

1 Afghanistan (2001–15). A war fought to close down terrorist training camps used by Al Qaeda.
2 The Iraq War (2003–11). Inspired by **neoconservative** thinking, this was an attempt to spread democracy to the Middle East.

With the USA fighting two further wars not dissimilar in some ways to Vietnam, Vietnam itself became a 'live' issue.

1990s

The decade began with two dramatic events:

1 The Gulf War (1991). An American-led coalition defeated the Iraqi army with minimal US casualties. President Bush announced that the ghost of Vietnam had been laid to rest.
2 The fall of the Soviet Union (1991). The USSR broke up into many states, leaving the Russian Federation as the 'rump' of the old Soviet Empire. America had won the Cold War, but in the background radical Islam was growing in the Middle East.

These events led historians to reassess Vietnam as a war that contributed to the defeat of the Soviet Union.

1980s

President Reagan replaced Carter in 1981 and set out to restore American prestige. American forces went into limited, small-scale action in Granada, in the Gulf of Sirte and in Lebanon. Reagan referred to Vietnam as a 'noble cause', encouraging historians to reassess the war in the light of Soviet adventurism in Afghanistan. The Cold War came to an end with the fall of the Berlin Wall (1989). Revisionism was greatly encouraged by the evidence that communism was being defeated as an ideology.

1970s

America withdrew from Vietnam (1973) and South Vietnam fell to the communists (1975). Reeling from defeat, the USA was reluctant to commit troops to a combat role. In 1979 President Carter tried and failed to rescue American diplomats taken hostage in Iran. His failure reinforced the image of America as weak, which encouraged the USSR to invade Afghanistan (1979). Tentatively, the first 'revisionist' texts appeared.

Impact on Vietnam War historiography		
Orthodox arguments	**Military revisionism**	**Political revisionism**
		The End of History and the Last Man by Francis Fukuyama (1992). Argued that America's victory in the Cold War proved that democracy and capitalism were the inevitable end product of history.
	On Strategy: A Critical Analysis of the Vietnam War by Harry Summers (1982). Claimed that America's leaders in the 1960s failed to grasp elementary principles of warfare.	
The Best and Brightest by David Halberstam (1972). Formed the bedrock of orthodox thinking by its criticism of Kennedy and Johnson and their advisors.		*America in Vietnam* by Guenter Lewy (1978). Questioned the orthodox view by arguing that America's credibility was at stake in Vietnam.

Seeds of division

The Vietnam War was probably the most divisive American event of the twentieth century. This is a bold claim. After the First World War there was a long and bitter national debate over America's declaration of war on Germany, from which emerged the isolationism that contributed – by America's absence – to the outbreak of the Second World War. But the arguments over the Great War became irrelevant when the Japanese attacked Pearl Harbor in December 1941. Thereafter the United States abandoned isolationism and became a global superpower.

By contrast, the Vietnam War revealed fissures running through American society, some of which have grown deeper with the passage of time. The war divided America in every possible way. For example, the **baby boomers** were by no means united in their opposition to the war. Many young Americans volunteered to serve in Vietnam, or accepted conscription without complaint. Americans of all ages began arguing over the meaning of patriotism: conservatives accused antiwar protestors of being unpatriotic, while opponents of the war argued that they were trying to save America and its reputation.

Arguments about Vietnam were bitter and divisive from the start. Any historian wishing to develop a point of view only has to reach back into the Vietnam era to find evidence to support his or her argument. It is a mistake to assume that historians somehow know better than other people – they may have more accurate and extensive factual knowledge, but their judgements are affected by their reading of these facts, and by a host of other influences – current affairs, their political views, new evidence that comes to light through research, maybe even their religious, ethnic and social background.

In this chapter we will consider two ways of looking at the Vietnam War:

- the academic debate among historians
- the public and popular memory of the war, including the way it is depicted in films and the media.

Revisionism has challenged the orthodox interpretation, but it has not yet displaced it. Most historians still believe that the war was a mistake and that America could not have won it. One of the reasons revisionist history may never displace the orthodox interpretation is because it is, by definition, built on counterfactual arguments. *What if...* America had done this instead of that? *What if...* President Johnson had fought the war more vigorously? *What if...* President Kennedy had not colluded with the overthrow of President Ngo Dinh Diem in 1963? Arguments over the Vietnam War will certainly continue to divide historians into the foreseeable future.

The public and popular memory of the war

In one of the greatest American films of the 1970s, Martin Scorsese's *Taxi Driver*, there is a veiled reference to Vietnam. Robert De Niro's character has gone for a job interview. In the course of the interview, he is asked whether he has any skills. After a moment's hesitation he replies, 'I'm

Baby boomers
Children born in the 15 years or so after the Second World War.

good with crowds.' To American audiences in the 1970s this was a very menacing statement. De Niro's character Travis Bickel is a Vietnam veteran. He is also a psychopath.

The traumatised Vietnam veteran is one of the standard images of the public mind. He appears in numerous films – *Rambo: First Blood, Lethal Weapon, Rolling Thunder* – usually as an indestructible angel of vengeance employing his skills to wage war on American criminals. In *Jarhead* a dishevelled Vietnam veteran greets Marines returning victorious from the Gulf War of 1991, a reference to the psychological damage inflicted by Vietnam.

In the real world, outside of Hollywood, there is widespread recognition that the war deeply affected its participants. Post-traumatic stress disorder is recognised today as a diagnosable condition affecting tens of thousands of Vietnam veterans, but many left the military with 'other-than-honourable' discharges before the condition was recognised, affecting their employment prospects and welfare benefits. This has led to lawsuits in which veterans attempt to force the Defence Department to upgrade their discharges, which it is reluctant to do. A similar problem surrounds veterans affected by Agent Orange, trying to prove that chemical defoliants caused their health problems.

The advent of the internet has led to the formation of hundreds of veterans' social networking sites across the country. There you will find ongoing discussions of these and other issues, and around Veterans' Day (11 November) there are hundreds of postings of photographs of Vietnam soldiers. The war is far from forgotten.

Inevitably, the legacy of the war has been used and abused in political debates, especially in the last two decades, when the Vietnam generation has come of age as political candidates. For example, in the 2004 election John Kerry, the Democratic candidate, was a Vietnam veteran who served in the US Navy on river patrol boats. He was awarded a Silver Star, a Bronze Star, and the **Purple Heart** three times. When he returned to the United States he became an outspoken critic of the war in Vietnam. During the election campaign his service record became the subject of intense scrutiny, particularly his three Purple Hearts. His critics pointed out that these did not necessarily suggest exceptional bravery, since they can be awarded for minor wounds and do not require an officer's citation to be awarded. The Republicans were casting doubt on his war record. Similarly, the Democrats pointed out that President George W. Bush served in the Texas Air National Guard during the Vietnam War, a unit that was unlikely to be sent into armed combat.

Probably the best place to evaluate the public's memory of the war is at the Vietnam Veterans' Memorial Wall in Washington. On any given day there you will find dozens of people who have come to pay their respects to fallen friends and relatives, to leave mementoes, flags, poems, prayers or flowers. We started Section 1 of this book with the wall, a 'story written in stone', and it seems an appropriate place to end it. But the story is also set in the love and grief of millions of people, in America, in Vietnam, in Australia, in Laos and Cambodia, whose lives were permanently altered by a war that is slowly receding into history.

Purple Heart
A medal awarded for being wounded or killed while in action against an enemy of the United States. If wounded, the wound must have required treatment by a medical officer resulting in an official record of treatment.

Vietnam War films

Insight

Many students' first encounter with Vietnam will be through Hollywood films. This could be unfortunate, because first impressions are often the most enduring. There is, of course, a sense in which these films could be regarded as primary sources – films released in the 1970s were based on scripts written while the war was still in progress, and many later films are based on first-hand accounts. However, all such films should be treated with caution. In the dog-eat-dog world of Hollywood, the urge to sensationalise is very powerful. Some misconceptions might become so widely held that it becomes almost impossible to dislodge them. For example, consider the following excerpt from an article by the Australian journalist John Pilger, in which he discusses the Russian roulette scene in *The Deer Hunter*:

At the level of popular culture … post-war propaganda has worked assiduously to celebrate the invader and to reduce the invaded to their wartime status of commie stick figures on celluloid. *The Deer Hunter* … was the first prime example … The film's dramatic pitch was reached during recurring orgiastic scenes in which the American heroes were forced to play Russian roulette by their Vietnamese captors. In all my time in Vietnam I never heard about this 'game'. I asked others who had been there if they had heard about it and they had not. Interviews with returning American prisoners-of-war never mentioned it, and these surely would have been seized upon at the time as confirmation of the enemy's inhumanity.

From 'A Noble Cause', in John Pilger, *Heroes* (1986)

It is unrealistic, however, to expect students of the Vietnam War not to watch these films. What is important is that, if you watch them, you should do so with a critical eye and an awareness of their place in time. With the exception of *Heaven and Earth*, what all of the following films have in common is that they portray the Americans as victims of the war. Hollywood tends to treat the Vietnam War as a disaster for the Americans, rather than for the Vietnamese.

The Green Berets (1968), dir. Roy Kellogg, John Wayne and Mervyn Le Roy

Disturbed by criticism of the war, John Wayne made a patriotic film in the tradition of his Second World War movies. The simple message is that communism is evil and the Americans are the good guys. Most memorable scene: Sergeant Petersen (Jim Hutton) steps on a booby trap, gets whisked into the air and skewered on a framework of bamboo spikes.

The 'first wave'

The first Hollywood films about the Vietnam War were looking for big truths about the human condition, something that would lift Vietnam above the ordinary genre of war movies. These films were self-consciously intellectual, more the product of professional Hollywood scriptwriters than Vietnam veterans.

Coming Home (1978), dir. Hal Ashby

With 'Hanoi Jane' in the leading role, this film was never going to appeal to conservative nationalists. Inspired by the story of Ron Kovic (see *Born on the Fourth of July*), the film focuses on the human wreckage of war. It was highly critical of the medical treatment available for wounded veterans, and like its Falklands War British equivalent (*Tumbledown* (1988), dir. Richard Eyre, starring Colin Firth) it was criticised as unpatriotic for opposing the war. Most memorable scene: Sally Hyde (Jane Fonda) makes love to the paralysed Luke Martin (Jon Voight).

98

The Deer Hunter (1978), dir. Michael Cimino

A film about friendship and love, in which good Americans help each other to survive the beastliness of the Vietnamese. A spiritual element is suggested by the hunting of deer in the Pennsylvania mountains, where a good clean shot brings you closer to God. No such thing as a good clean shot in Vietnam, unfortunately. Most memorable scene: Michael (Robert De Niro) and Nick (Christopher Walken) are forced to play Russian roulette by their Vietnamese captors.

My personal favourite Vietnam War film

Apocalypse Now (1979), dir. Francis Ford Coppola

Arguably the most famous Vietnam War movie, this film is based on Joseph Conrad's *Heart of Darkness*. The film was thought to be too controversial to make as long as American soldiers were fighting in Vietnam. Made in the Philippines, the leading actor (Martin Sheen) suffered a heart attack during the filming. Most memorable scene: American helicopters attack a communist stronghold.

Conrad's *Heart of Darkness* (1899) was seen as an appropriate metaphor for Vietnam as early as 1965. Conrad's novella is set in the Belgian Congo at the turn of the twentieth century, at the height of European imperialism. The main character and narrator of the story, Charles Marlow, is the captain of a river-steamboat employed by a company trading in ivory. He is sent up-river from the Company Station, near the river mouth, to the Central Station several hundred miles inland, where he discovers rumours concerning a Mr Kurtz at the Inner Station, far up the river in the heart of the Congo. During the long journey up-river Marlow and his crew pass from civilisation to barbarism.

Arriving at the Inner Station, Marlow is confronted by scenes of utter depravity and violence. Decapitated heads of natives adorn a row of posts near Kurtz's station house. The natives worship Kurtz as a god, and are prepared to do his every bidding. Kurtz himself is an ambiguous figure – highly intelligent, poetic, well educated, a man who gets things done – but also a man who has turned to terror, around whom all civilisation has collapsed. The longer Marlow stays at the Inner Station, the more he realises that his own sanity is at stake. Kurtz dies on the return journey. As he dies, Marlow hears his final whisper: 'The horror! The horror!'

Transposed for the Vietnam War, *Apocalypse Now* draws heavily on Conrad's story, not only for the plot but also for specific scenes. Marlow becomes Captain Willard, an American special operations officer sent up the Mekong River into Cambodia to assassinate his superior officer, Major Kurtz, who has gone insane. Travelling up-river in a Navy patrol boat, he and the crew experience a series of encounters that are progressively more bizarre and surreal. As in Conrad's novella, the closer they get to Kurtz, the further they are from civilisation and sanity. The closing scenes of the film – Willard's encounter with Kurtz – are one of cinema's epic dramas. The entire film is visually spectacular.

What makes *Apocalypse Now* stand out in a field of excellent films? It was based on a story written by one of the 'giants' of English literature. It was directed by one of Hollywood's greatest directors. It drew on Michael Herr's eyewitness account of the war (see page 40). It was acted by some of the greatest actors America has ever produced – Marlon Brando, Martin Sheen, Robert Duvall, Dennis Hopper. In my opinion, too, it captures the essence of what went wrong in Vietnam – a modern superpower misguidedly trying to impose freedom on a distant country and, in the process, bringing in its wake chaos, destruction and moral ambiguity.

The 'second wave'

In the late 1980s a new wave of Vietnam War films emerged that rejected profound philosophical meanings and focused on realism. Vietnam veterans had seen the films of the 'first wave' and, on reflection, decided that they were unrealistic.

Platoon (1986), dir. Oliver Stone

The first film in Oliver Stone's Vietnam War trilogy. Hailed in 1986 for its realism, the film turns on the dramatic conflict between two American sergeants, Barnes (Tom Berenger) and Elias (Willem Dafoe), whose mortal enmity reflects the dichotomy at the heart of the American war. Most memorable scene: Chris Taylor's (Charlie Sheen) first ambush.

Full Metal Jacket (1987), dir. Stanley Kubrick

Heavily influenced by Michael Herr's *Dispatches* (see page 40), this movie is unusual among Vietnam War films for the urban setting of its combat scenes, depicting the battle for Hue in 1968. Most memorable scene: Lee Ermey's performance as the Marine drill instructor.

Hamburger Hill (1987), dir. John Irvin

Based on a real incident, and noted for its realism, American infantry have to capture a fortified hill. In true Vietnam style, once taken the Americans abandon the hill. To Americans, the contrast between this battle and the Second World War battle for Mount Suribachi on Iwo Jima is profound. Most memorable scene: an American helicopter gunship wipes out the American soldiers leading the attack on the hilltop in a 'friendly fire' incident.

Born on the Fourth of July (1989), dir. Oliver Stone

The second film in Stone's Vietnam trilogy, this is based on the true story of Ron Kovic (Tom Cruise), an American soldier who volunteered for Vietnam and was paralysed from the waist down. Politicised by his experiences, he becomes a leading member of an antiwar group, Veterans Against the War. Most memorable scene: Ron Kovic disrupts President Nixon's Republican Party Convention during the 1972 presidential election.

Heaven and Earth (1993), dir. Oliver Stone

The final film in Stone's trilogy, this is one of the few films to view the war from the perspective of the Vietnamese, based on the true story of Le Ly Hayslip (Hiep Thi). Tortured by the South Vietnamese Army and raped by the Viet Cong, she meets an American sergeant (Tommy Lee Jones) who marries her and takes her back with him to America. There is to be no happy ending: her husband, affected by post-traumatic stress disorder, becomes violent and commits suicide. Most memorable scene: Le Ly's return to Vietnam to show her sons her former homeland.

A selection of widely differing films

Southern Comfort (1981), dir. Walter Hill

An allegory of the war, this is the story of a group of soldiers sent on exercises in the Louisiana Bayeu. A prank goes wrong when they open fire with blanks on a group of Cajun fishermen, who return fire with real ammunition. Lost in the swamps, the soldiers are hunted down and killed. This is the cinematic version of the 'quagmire' theory, with the Americans 'in over their heads'. Most memorable scene: Spencer (Keith Carradine) and Hardin (Powers Boothe) find themselves fighting for survival during a Cajun ho-down.

Rambo: First Blood (1982), dir. George P. Cosmatos

There are several justifications for including *Rambo* in this list of Vietnam War films. Firstly, John Rambo's psychotic violence is supposedly a reaction to his Vietnam experiences. Secondly, the film reflected an American reaction to Vietnam similar to that of many Germans after the Great War – the myth of the Great Betrayal. Rambo (aka America) is clearly invincible, therefore he must have been 'stabbed in the back'. The film played an important part in the psychological rejection of defeat during the Reagan presidency. Most memorable scene: Rambo (Sylvester Stallone) destroys a town with a .50 calibre machine gun.

A Bright Shining Lie (1998), dir. Terry George

A made-for-television film based on the book of the same name by Neil Sheehan, this film offers the most comprehensive explanation of the American defeat despite its lack of Hollywood polish. Most memorable scene: John Paul Vann (Bill Paxton) calls in a B-52 strike on his own position during the fighting around Kontum in 1972.

We Were Soldiers (2001), dir. Randall Wallace

Based on the book *We Were Soldiers Once … and Young* by Lt Gen Harold Moore, the film tells the story of the Battle of the Ia Drang Valley. Most memorable scene: Lt Col Moore's wife Julie (Madeleine Stowe) delivering Western Union telegrams to the wives of soldiers who have been killed.

Rescue Dawn (2006), dir. Werner Herzog

Based on a true story, *Rescue Dawn* brings the genre of Vietnam War films back to its starting point – the beastliness of the communists, and how good it is to be an American. An American pilot shot down on an (illegal) mission over Laos falls into the hands of the Pathet Lao and escapes back to civilisation. Most memorable scene: Duane Martin (Steve Zahn) is beheaded by Laotian villagers.

Insight

Introduction to Chapters 7 and 8

Before Vietnam – The USA in Asia after 1945

In the first six chapters of this book we have explored the Vietnam War – its causes, the fighting and some of its consequences within the United States. The student of history, however, needs to be able to place Vietnam in the broader thread of time in order to better understand its importance. Section 2 therefore focuses on the historical context in which Vietnam needs to be understood. Much of this context has been briefly mentioned, including the Cold War and the American policy of containment to halt the spread of communism, but now needs to be explored in more detail. Therefore Chapters 7 and 8 focus on:

Chapter 7: How the Cold War spread to Asia, 1945–51

Chapter 8: The Korean War, 1950–53

Chapters 7 and 8 demonstrate that the USA's experiences in Asia proved very different from what had been expected and hoped for in 1945 when the USA was very optimistic about its future in Asia. This introduction (pages 102–104)

△ An American naval task force at anchor at Majuro Atoll, 1944. This photograph gives some idea of the size of the US fleet in the Pacific Ocean by the end of the war. Victory in the Second World War turned the Pacific into an American lake.

therefore focuses on what the United States hoped to achieve in Asia after the defeat of Japan in 1945, providing the context for the problems that arose so quickly afterwards.

Victory in the Pacific

On 7 December 1941 the Japanese navy attacked Pearl Harbor, bringing America into the Second World War. The destruction of the American fleet at Pearl Harbor cleared the way for Japan's war of conquest in Asia. In the following months the Japanese captured a vast empire to add to the conquests they'd made in China since 1937 – Burma and Malaya, the Dutch East Indies and across the Pacific Ocean as far as New Guinea and the Marshall Islands. To do this they had to take the Philippines, which meant war with America. Japan's early victories also had a powerful psychological effect throughout Asia: the fact that an Asian power had humiliated Britain, France and America destroyed the myth of Western invincibility.

American forces turned the tide of the Pacific War in 1942 in two critical battles. At Midway Island the US Navy destroyed four of the Japanese aircraft carriers that had attacked Pearl Harbor, killing Japan's most experienced naval pilots; from Midway onwards the Japanese were on the defensive. At Guadalcanal the US Army halted the spread of Japanese forces and began the 'island-hopping' campaign across the Pacific that brought them, in 1945, to Iwo Jima and Okinawa. The capture of these islands brought the Japanese mainland within range of American bombers. In 1944 General Douglas MacArthur recaptured the Philippines at the head of the American army fighting its way back from Australia through New Guinea and the Indies towards Japan.

By 1945 Japan was assailed on all sides. In Burma the British liberated large swathes of territory, pinning down forces that could have been used elsewhere. American submarines destroyed Japanese merchant ships, imposing a blockade that brought Japan's economy to its knees. Day after day American B-29 bombers firebombed Japanese cities, while the US Navy fought off swarms of kamikaze aircraft. Then in August 1945 the United States dropped atomic bombs on Hiroshima and Nagasaki. Days later the American fleet dropped anchor in Tokyo Bay and Japan surrendered. To drive home the enormity of Japan's defeat, 400 B-29 bombers and 1,500 carrier planes flew overhead after the surrender ceremony on board the US battleship *Missouri*.

By the end of the war American military power in the Pacific Ocean was enormous. The US Navy was larger than all the other navies of the world combined: there were over 50 American aircraft carriers in the Pacific, supported by an enormous fleet of battleships, cruisers, destroyers and auxiliary ships. The American Army was battle-hardened, supported by the economic power of American industry. With no obvious enemies in the Far East, American prestige was at its zenith. It seemed that the Far East was an empty page, ready for America to write the script of its next stage of development. Central to American hopes were the countries of China and Japan, although they were undergoing very different experiences. China was in the midst of a civil war in which it would decide its own future. Japan, totally defeated, waited to see what fate lay in store for it.

What did the USA want in China after 1945?

Ever since the nineteenth century American policy-makers had dreamed of what they called the 'open door' in China. The Chinese mainland had always been closed to foreign businesses but, with a population of over 400 million people, China was a vast potential market for American manufactured goods. During the twentieth century the fulfilment of this dream had been delayed by a series of catastrophic events in China – the Chinese revolution, the

Chinese civil war that followed, and the Japanese invasion of China. In 1945 the Chinese civil war was still going on, but America's ally, the nationalist leader Chiang Kai-shek, appeared to have a good chance of defeating Mao Zedong's communists now that the Japanese were gone. If the nationalists (Kuomintang) could win the civil war, the dream of an 'open door' to China might come true. However, US hopes would be thwarted if the communists came to power.

The American occupation of Japan

The United States had great hopes of building Western-style capitalism across the Far East, strengthened by democratically elected governments and Western institutions. The cornerstone of this policy of Americanisation was Japan which, in 1941, had been ruled by a hereditary emperor and governed by the Army and was a deeply traditional, religious country. In 1945 Japan faced considerable change now that it was occupied by American forces and governed by the Supreme Command of the Allied Forces (SCAP), headed by the supreme commander himself, General Douglas MacArthur.

The Japanese mainland was occupied by US troops because the Allies had agreed during the war to treat Japan like Germany, dividing it into occupation zones administered by each of the interested powers. However, the Soviet Union was not at war with Japan, and did not declare war until August 1945, by which time the Americans were in possession of the atomic bomb and no longer needed – or wanted – Soviet help. When Japan surrendered, the Americans occupied the four main islands – Honshu, Hokkaido, Shikoku and Kyushu – along with southern Korea. The Soviet Union hastily declared war and occupied northern Korea, Sakhalin and the Kurile Islands to the north of Japan, China took control of Taiwan, and Britain occupied Hong Kong and the Solomon Islands. Thus America took the dominant role in the occupation of mainland Japan.

In 1945 America's policy in Japan was to create a 'model state', a pure democracy that would form the blueprint for spreading Western democratic capitalism into Asia. The US

Government saw Japan like a ball of clay, ready to be moulded to suit America's needs. MacArthur set about transforming Japan into a Westernised, capitalist, democratic state.

The aim of these reforms, in the words of the historian Kenneth Thomson, was to 'throw a fast ball into the catcher's mitt that is Asia'. Reformed Japan would become the springboard for spreading liberal democracy across the Far East. With it would come the investment opportunities and free markets that would hopefully one day bind both shores of the 'American lake' in a mutually beneficial capitalist handshake across the Pacific Ocean.

The ambitious nature of these reforms suggests how confident the USA felt in 1945. However, events in Japan and other parts of Asia did not take place in isolation. They were to be affected by the outcome of the civil war in China and by the spread of the Cold War from Europe. Those high hopes were about to take a pounding.

De-mystifying the emperor
Before the war Emperor Hirohito was a god-like figure, his title so sacred that there was no word for 'emperor' in Japanese. The first time most Japanese heard their emperor's voice was on 15 August 1945, when he announced Japan's unconditional surrender on the radio. This was a huge shock, followed by the sight of photographs of the immaculate Hirohito standing beside MacArthur, who was dressed casually, with no tie and in standard uniform.

Democratisation
Before the war Japan was governed under the Meiji constitution, a highly aristocratic, conservative government that concentrated power in the hands of an imperial elite. Now a new American-style constitution transferred sovereignty from the emperor to the people of Japan. Japan would be governed by a prime minister and a democratically elected parliament. Women were given the vote for the first time and a bill of rights guaranteed fundamental liberties. The emperor was reduced to a symbolic head of state.

Pacification
The new constitution contained a 'no war, no arms' clause that said that Japan could not maintain a standing army. War was no longer acceptable as an instrument of state policy – Japan was to be a pacifist state. The Shinto religion, seen as militaristic and nationalistic, was no longer Japan's official faith. War crimes tribunals sentenced a number of men to death or imprisonment for planning aggressive war or for crimes against civilians and prisoners.

How did General MacArthur intend to change Japan after 1945?

Liberalising the economy
Old Japan was a highly conservative society dominated by strict social codes. The Americans promoted liberal social change. Free-market competition was encouraged in the economy: Japanese industry was to be broken up from its pre-war monopolies and large conglomerates ('zaibatsu') that were thought to have contributed to its aggressive foreign policy. Land reform saw property purchased from landlords and sold at low prices to farmers to liberate them from serfdom.

Education
Before the war Japan's education system aimed at educating an elite for government and military service. After the war the system was reformed to resemble the American system of high schools. The aim was to make opportunities available to all students regardless of their social origins. Japan was to be a meritocracy, a country in which people born in the lower ranks of society could rise as far as their abilities might take them.

△ Hirohito, Emperor of Japan, 1942

▽ General Douglas MacArthur, 24 August, 1945

7 Why did the USA believe the communists were responsible for spreading the Cold War to Asia, 1945–51?

The 'reverse course' in Japan

In 1947 a profound change occurred in American policy in Japan. For two years MacArthur's Government had been working hard to turn Japan into a nation that completely rejected the use of force. Japan's armed forces had been disbanded and Japanese industry was banned from producing war materials. The 'zaibatsu' – the monopolies and large industrial conglomerates that dominated Japan's economy in the 1930s – were being broken up to liberalise the economy and encourage competition. Japanese soldiers accused of war crimes were being put on trial. Then suddenly in 1947 the USA put these changes into reverse. Economic power was handed back to Japanese businesses, the same conservatives who had always run Japan's industries. War crimes trials quickly abated. Many administrators and soldiers who had served the Imperial Japanese government were brought back into power. Japanese industry once again began to manufacture weapons and ammunition – using American raw materials. This abrupt change of policy is called the 'reverse course'.

Why did the United States change course in Japan? Part of the explanation simply lies within Japan itself. MacArthur's Government was facing an economic crisis brought about by the widespread wartime destruction and the dislocation of Japanese industry resulting from the liberalisation programme. Furthermore, Japan still faced the fundamental problem of its economy: being volcanic, Japan's islands lacked the raw materials – the coal, oil and iron ore – needed to sustain economic growth. But the main reason for the 'reverse course' was because the Cold War was coming to Asia.

By 1947 US analysts were warning of the likely victory of the communists in the Chinese civil war, a development that would threaten America's entire Asian policy. Within three years America's worst fears were realised:

- In 1949 the communists won the Chinese civil war and America's wartime ally, Chiang Kai-shek, fled with his nationalist Chinese army to the island of Formosa.

- That same year the Soviet Union exploded its own atomic bomb, ending the American monopoly of nuclear weapons.

- In 1950 communist North Korea invaded South Korea, drawing the USA and its UN allies into a new (and very unpopular) war in the Far East.

- When American forces invaded North Korea and approached the Chinese border, communist China intervened in the war and attacked the Americans and their allies.

Date	Event	Impact of event
December 1941	Japan attacked Pearl Harbor	Shocked America out of its isolationism and brought the USA into the Second World War
1945	USA dropped atomic bombs on Japanese cities of Hiroshima and Nagasaki	Ended the Second World War signalled to the Soviet Union that the USA possessed nuclear weapons and was prepared to use them
	Occupation of Japan by US forces	USA began transforming Japan into a Western-style liberal democracy
	Marshall mission to China began	Failure of mission to prevent a communist victory in China in 1949 helped to start the Red Scare and the McCarthy era in the USA
1946	George Kennan's 'long telegram' from Moscow to the US Government	Warned the US Government of the inherently aggressive nature of Soviet communism
1947	President Truman's 'Truman Doctrine' speech	Truman committed the USA to the policy of containment of communism
	'Reverse course' in Japan	Indicated that US fears of communist influence in the Far East were growing
1949	Communists under Mao Zedong won the civil war in China Nationalists under Chiang Kai-shek fled to Formosa	Seen in the USA as a catastrophic failure of US foreign policy Nationalist occupation of Formosa created a permanent communist Chinese grievance, against Formosa itself but also against the USA for supporting it
	USSR exploded its first atomic bomb	Ended the American monopoly in nuclear weapons and contributed to the anticommunist 'witch hunt' in the USA
1950	NSC-68 produced by the US National Security Council	Reinforced the policy of containment led to a massive increase in US defence expenditure
	North Korea invaded South Korea	Led to the Korean War; Cold War had spread to Asia Confirmed US suspicions of communist intentions, thus also reinforcing the domino theory in Vietnam

■ **Enquiry Focus:** Why did the USA believe the communists were responsible for spreading the Cold War to Asia?

1 Read the sections (below) on the factors that contributed to the Cold War spreading to Asia:

- Soviet expansionism
- The US strategy of the 'defensive perimeter'
- The communist victory in the Chinese civil war and the political reaction in the United States
- US economic and commercial expansion into Asia.

Soviet expansionism

For much of the period since the 1950s the story of how the Cold War spread to Asia has been told through the orthodox interpretation, which says that Soviet expansionism was the root cause of the Asiatic Cold War, with the communists seeking to extend their ideology and influence into Asia, and the United States setting out a defensive strategy of containment. Why did the USA believe in communist expansionism?

In 1945 most Americans believed that the world was now a much safer place. Their forces had played a major part in defeating Nazi Germany and Japan and the world crisis seemed over. The coming of the Cold War, first in Europe and then in the Far East, has been described by one historian as 'the return of fear' as America struggled to face up to the new communist threat.

The focus of American concerns was the Soviet Union. In 1946 an American diplomat in Moscow, George Kennan, sent a 'long telegram' to the US Government. Kennan, who had experience of Stalin's Russia dating back to the early 1930s, warned America of the nature of the Soviet threat, and called upon the USA to assume leadership of the free world. By 1947 Kennan's 'long telegram' was public knowledge and was helping to reshape American attitudes towards their former ally. In a subsequent article called 'The Sources of Soviet Conduct', Kennan recommended:

In these circumstances it is clear that the main element of any United States policy toward the Soviet Union must be that of long-term, patient but firm and vigilant containment of Russian expansive tendencies ... The Soviet pressure against the free institutions of the western world is something that can be contained by the adroit and vigilant application of counter-force at a series of constantly shifting geographical and political points, corresponding to the shifts and manoeuvres of Soviet policy...

In 1950 members of America's intelligence community, the National Security Council, drafted NSC-68, a document that confirmed the logic of Kennan's telegram, but warned that the threat was not confined to Europe.

NSC-68 offered a detailed analysis of Soviet intentions and resources, explaining that, by its very nature, the Soviet regime had to continue territorial expansion in order to survive. This did not necessarily mean expanding the frontiers of the Soviet Union: the USSR could spread its influence and ideology into other parts of the world left vulnerable by the Second World War. This particularly applied to the Far East, where the Japanese victories of the 1930s and early 1940s had destroyed the old presumption of the superiority of Europeans over Asiatic peoples. The following extract warns of the likely consequences of failing to contain communism at an early stage:

> The shadow of Soviet force falls darkly on Western Europe and Asia and supports [the theory of a Soviet] policy of encroachment. The free world lacks adequate means – in the form of forces in being – to thwart such expansion locally. The United States will therefore be confronted more frequently with the dilemma of reacting totally [i.e. by war] to a limited extension of Soviet control or of not reacting at all. Continuation of present trends is likely to lead, therefore, to a gradual withdrawal under the direct or indirect pressure of the Soviet Union, until we discover one day that we have sacrificed positions of vital interest.

NSC-68 may be seen as the real origin of the policy of containment, for although President Truman committed the USA to a broad doctrine, NSC-68 laid down in detail the blueprint of how it should work in practice. In some ways the document was optimistic: it argued that the economic and potential military forces of the Western world were superior to those of the USSR, but it warned that it often took the West time to respond to major acts of aggression. The existence of Soviet nuclear weapons, however, made Western lack of preparedness far more risky.

NSC-68 concluded that America's best course of action was to confront the spread of communism with 'a rapid build-up of political, economic, and military strength in the free world', so that the West was not caught by surprise by future communist aggression. Of particular importance was the concept of strengthening the will and the means to resist communism in vulnerable regions like the Far East. Herein lies the origin of the assumption that all communist activity was orchestrated and supported by the Soviet Union, a monolithic view of world communism that finally came to grief in the rice paddies and jungles of South Vietnam.

The defensive perimeter strategy in the Far East

By 1950 the United States was constructing a defensive perimeter in the Far East to hold back the threat of communism. In the nineteenth century the 'open door' policy was driven mainly by the hope that the vast potential market of China could be opened up to American business. By the 1950s, however, the emphasis had shifted to the vast economic resources of the region, resources that had to be denied to the Soviet Union and its Chinese ally in the new struggle for world domination. The map on the next page shows how the Far East looked to American policy-makers in the 1950s and how they sought to apply the principles of NSC-68 to that region.

◁ The defensive perimeter: American strategy in the Far East focused on creating a defensive perimeter to contain the expansion of communism. In 1951 the ANZUS Pact guaranteed the defence of Australia and New Zealand. In 1955 the United States organised the South East Asian Treaty Organisation (SEATO) involving Britain, France, Australia, New Zealand, the Philippines, Siam and Pakistan, to prevent the spread of communism in Southeast Asia.

If you turn the map upside down, you can see why communist China saw the American strategy as aggressive, with Formosa pointing at the heart of the Chinese mainland. To the Americans, Formosa represented the true, legitimate government of China; to the communist Chinese, Formosa was the dangerous counter-revolutionary alter ego of China, occupying its seat in the United Nations.

The communist victory in the Chinese civil war, 1949

No event shocked the US Government and the American public more than the victory of the communists in the Chinese civil war. As we saw above (page 103) America was keen to see China opened up to foreign trade and investment. With American industry spearheading mass production techniques, businessmen looked to China for a vast, open market for American manufactured goods, but this was only likely to come about if the Chinese nationalist forces won the civil war against the Chinese communists.

The story of American policy towards China from the 1940s can be told through the patches, the cloth insignia worn by the American military. They illustrate US policies and a range of emotions, from optimism through hope and diplomacy to confrontation and war.

From 1942 to 1945 the patch shown first was the US Army's China, Burma, India patch. America supported General Chiang Kai-shek and his nationalist Kuomintang forces against the Japanese in China, with the American General Stilwell acting as Chiang Kai-shek's liaison officer. To support nationalist forces in China, America sent supplies via India across the Himalayan mountains by air. It was a dangerous mission, with mixed results: with US help the nationalists stabilised the front in China, but

△ **Army patch of the China, Burma, India theatre.**

△ **Army patch of the Marshall mission to China.**

were unable to make headway against the Japanese until they surrendered in August 1945. The Americans hoped that victory over Japan would then enable Chiang Kai-shek to defeat the Chinese communists or, if that were impossible, to reach an agreement with them that would prevent Mao Zedong from forming an alliance with the Soviet Union.

The second patch is that of the Marshall mission to China. In late 1945 General George C. Marshall led an American military and diplomatic visit to China aimed at preventing a communist victory in the Chinese civil war. He hoped to forge an alliance between Chiang Kai-shek's nationalists, Mao Zedong's communists and the Americans to preserve China's independence from the Soviet Union. It was a dream that could not be realised: when the communists won the civil war in 1949, Chiang Kai-shek and the remnants of the nationalist army fled to Formosa (Taiwan) where they set up a rival government-in-exile. For the next quarter of a century the American Government refused to recognise the communists as the legitimate Government of China.

The final patch shown is of the 1st Marine Division. On 15 September 1950, during the Korean War, the Marines spearheaded a dangerous amphibious landing on the Inchon peninsula, near Seoul in South Korea. Just five years after defeating

Japan, the United States found itself fighting a war against communist China in Korea. America's worst fears seemed to be coming true. From 1950 until 1953 the American and allied armies were fought to a standstill in a conflict that threatened to escalate into an all-out war between China and the United States.

Why had the USA not been able to prevent the communist victory? The US secretary of state, Dean Acheson, gave this verdict in his White Paper on China in August 1949:

△ **Military patch of the 1st Marine Division.**

The unfortunate but inescapable fact is that the ominous result of the civil war in China was beyond the control of the government of the United States. Nothing that this country did or could have done within the reasonable limits of its capabilities could have changed that result; nothing that was left undone by this country has contributed to it. It was the product of internal Chinese forces, forces which this country tried to influence, but could not.

Many Americans, however, could not comprehend how America's Far East policy had gone so disastrously wrong. Fearful of communist influence in the American Government, the McCarthy 'witch hunt' of the early 1950s therefore targeted suspected communists and their 'fellow travellers', and sought scapegoats for the so-called failures of American policy. On 14 June 1951 Senator Joseph McCarthy delivered a speech to the Senate in which he said:

How can we account for our present situation unless we believe that men high in this Government are concerting to deliver us to disaster? This must be the product of a great conspiracy, a conspiracy on a scale so immense as to dwarf any previous such venture in the history of man. A conspiracy of infamy so black that, when it is finally exposed, its principals shall be forever deserving of the maledictions of all honest men ... It was [General] Marshall, with [Dean] Acheson eagerly assisting, who created the China policy which, destroying China, robbed us of a great and friendly ally, a buffer against the Soviet imperialism with which we are now at war.

McCarthy's words exemplify the extreme reactions in the USA to the communist victory in China and Chinese intervention in the Korean War, events that contributed to the anticommunist hysteria known as the Red Scare and the McCarthy era. General Marshall himself and the US Army were victimised by McCarthy and his supporters. The virulence of this domestic reaction can only be explained by the way people's high hopes and expectations had been dashed by the turn of events in the Far East.

US economic and commercial expansion into Asia

So far in this chapter the story of how the Cold War spread to Asia has been told through the orthodox interpretation that sees Soviet expansionism as the root cause of the Asiatic Cold War. Since the 1970s revisionist historians have challenged that interpretation. Many of the debates surrounding American policy in the Far East reflect the pattern of Vietnam historiography. For example, a new generation of historians more familiar with Asian languages and sources began detailed research into the culture and politics of Asian countries affected by US policy.

One argument, heavily influenced by the 'mistakes' of Vietnam, was that the USA was responsible for the extension of the Cold War to Asia because it sought to extend its economic and commercial empire into the region. This was a form of imperialist expansion – the search to secure raw materials, markets for American goods and investment opportunities for American business. This 'Coca-Cola' thesis became popular in the 1970s as critics of the Vietnam War drew inspiration from America's communist enemies and their interpretation of American behaviour. However, this 'revision' of the orthodox interpretation has failed to dislodge it. No historians working today entirely blame the United States for the fact that the Cold War spread to Asia, and many still lay the lion's share of that blame on the Soviet Union and communist China. Therefore, although the original American view of communist responsibility has been modified in many particulars through research, the orthodox view still commands academic respect.

■ Concluding your enquiry

In the winter of 1950–51, during the early phase of the Korean War, 300,000 Chinese soldiers, attacking in human waves, pursued an American army down the Korean peninsula. In the words of one American historian of the Cold War, John Lewis Gaddis, it was the 'most humiliating military reversal since the Civil War'. America's dream of expanding free-market capitalism and liberal democracy into the Far East had turned decidedly sour. By now it was clear that the Cold War had come to Asia with a vengeance.

1 Now that you have completed your notes, summarise the contribution of each factor on a mind map like the one on the right.

2 Use your mind map and your notes to plan and write an essay answering the question: why did the USA believe that the communists were responsible for spreading the Cold War to Asia, 1945–51?

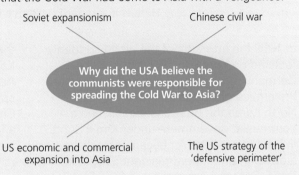

Soviet expansionism

Chinese civil war

Why did the USA believe the communists were responsible for spreading the Cold War to Asia?

US economic and commercial expansion into Asia

The US strategy of the 'defensive perimeter'

8 Was the Korean War 'a rehearsal for Vietnam'?

Here is a standard narrative of the Korean War, written for a GCSE class:

In 1950 the attention of the world suddenly focused on Korea. In 1945 Korea – like Germany – had been cut in half by the armies of Russia and America. In North Korea the Russians established a communist government under Kim il Sung. In South Korea the Americans established a government under President Syngman Rhee. Both the Americans and the Russians withdrew their forces from Korea by 1950.

In 1950 North Korea invaded the South, and soon only the city of Pusan was holding out against the North (see the first map). President Truman was convinced that the invasion threatened the free world, and sent American forces to help South Korea. The United Nations passed a resolution to send troops as well – the USSR was unable to veto the resolution because it was boycotting the UN at that time.

The UN forces landed at Inchon in September 1950, threatening to cut the North Koreans' supply and communications. The North Koreans were quickly forced out of South Korea. The situation was now very dangerous. Should the UN follow up its victory and invade North Korea? In October the UN crossed the 38th parallel into North Korea. Soon its forces, commanded by the American General Douglas MacArthur, were spreading towards the border with China. The Chinese warned that they would not stand by and watch the Americans defeat North Korea (see the second map).

MacArthur was ordered by Truman not to provoke Chinese intervention. However, MacArthur ordered UN forces to the Yalu River in pursuit of North Korean troops. Thousands of Chinese soldiers poured into Korea to attack the UN forces, which were driven south in a panic-stricken retreat (see the third map). MacArthur was sacked by Truman.

For the next three years Korea was devastated by war. Neither side could win: the UN had the advantages of air superiority and total naval supremacy, but the Chinese had unlimited manpower. The fighting stabilised along a line near the 38th parallel until 1953, when a truce was signed. Korea was once again divided along the 38th parallel (see the fourth map). Some 5 million people had been killed or wounded, and the economy of Korea had suffered severe damage. Both sides claimed victory.

A simple narrative like the one you have just read serves a useful purpose: already you know what the Korean War was and the broad outline of events. It explains why Korea is still divided today – there was no peace treaty, so officially North and South Korea are still at war. But a narrative like this also has its limitations. With your knowledge of the Vietnam War you should be able to ask lots of questions and make comparisons. Why was Korea split in two after 1945? What kind of leaders were Kim il Sung and Syngman Rhee? Why, with all its technology and firepower, did the United States not defeat North Korea and its Chinese allies?

It does not appear too difficult to write a brief narrative history of the Korean War. How difficult would it be to do the same for Vietnam?

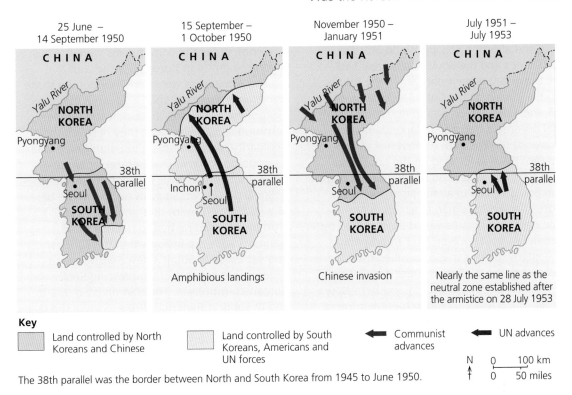

25 June – 14 September 1950	15 September – 1 October 1950	November 1950 – January 1951	July 1951 – July 1953
	Amphibious landings	Chinese invasion	Nearly the same line as the neutral zone established after the armistice on 28 July 1953

Key

▨ Land controlled by North Koreans and Chinese

▨ Land controlled by South Koreans, Americans and UN forces

◄ Communist advances

◄ UN advances

N   0   100 km
↑   0   50 miles

The 38th parallel was the border between North and South Korea from 1945 to June 1950.

■ Enquiry Focus: Was the Korean War 'a rehearsal for Vietnam'?

The Korean War did not last as long as the Vietnam War, nor did it leave as big a mark, so it is often called 'the forgotten war'. Yet in many ways, the Korean War was a huge war that deserves serious analysis. In this chapter we are going to subject Korea to that analysis by comparing and contrasting it to Vietnam.

Your task is to build an answer to the enquiry question above, analysing the similarities and differences between the two wars. To do this you are going to examine six key issues:

1 Why the Korean War started

2 Military aspects of the war

3 Disagreements among American leaders about how the war should be fought

4 The domestic reaction in the USA

5 How the war ended

6 The historiography of the Korean War.

When you have studied each issue, you will be given two statements. Statement A will be a statement about Korea that is too simplistic. Your first task will be to show that you understand how complex the issue is by adding the necessary qualifications, amendments and extra details, so that your finished statement about Korea is closer to the truth.

When you have done that, look at Statement B comparing Korea with the Vietnam War. Your second task will be to decide whether or not you agree with this statement. Give your reasons for agreeing or disagreeing with it in your notes.

Finally, on your own copy of the slide-line below, place each item where you think it should go, from 'Similar to Vietnam' to 'Different from Vietnam'. When you have done this for all six key issues, you should be ready to write an essay to answer the main question: was the Korean War 'a rehearsal for Vietnam'?

Similar to Vietnam   Different from Vietnam

◄————┼————————┼————————┼————————┼————————►

1. Why the Korean War started

During and after the Second World War the United States and the Soviet Union reached some important agreements about the future of Korea. Initially in the Cairo Declaration of 1943, the Allies agreed that in due course Korea would become a free and independent state. However, at the Potsdam Conference in July 1945 the USA was focused on the enormous task of invading Japan and needed Soviet help. When Stalin agreed to attack Japanese forces in Korea, the USA seemed to accept that the whole Korean peninsula would be occupied by the Soviet Army. However, after the dropping of the atomic bombs made an Allied invasion unnecessary, the US Government decided that American forces should occupy southern Korea after all. The Soviets agreed to halt their forces at the 38th parallel, and the Americans occupied the south. Then in December 1945 at a foreign ministers' conference in Moscow the Allies agreed that Korea should be governed for five years by a Four-Power International Trusteeship to prepare for reunification. That reunification never happened.

As in Vietnam, the Americans used the Japanese Army to maintain order in South Korea. The Japanese warned the Americans of the influence communists had among Koreans who had fought against the Japanese occupation. The largest and most popular political grouping was the Korean People's Republic (KPR). Many of the KPR were communist sympathisers imprisoned by the Japanese but – as in Vietnam – the Americans made little attempt to understand why communism was attractive to peasants living in a feudal society. When the Americans appointed a South Korean Interim Government, over half its members had been office-holders under the Japanese. The hated National Police that had supported Japanese tyranny in Korea were now equipped with American weapons to support the US military government, which suppressed the KPR in favour of the less popular Korean Democratic Republic, a right-wing movement led by Syngman Rhee.

In the North, the Soviet Union installed a communist government under the rule of Kim il Sung. Stalin was probably confident that free elections in Korea would return a communist government, as the communists were the best organised group in Korea after the war.

The Americans were convinced of the same thing: as in Vietnam, the USA feared that free elections would result in reunification under communist rule. However, they believed the popularity of communism in South Korea was a temporary consequence of the Japanese occupation: given time, non-communist political parties would grow and form the basis of a new government. But time was short. Truman believed he had to make a stand against Soviet expansionism in the Far East, and set about building a new South Korean government capable of suppressing South Korean communists. The USA decided that it had to support Syngman Rhee, despite the fact that he was a right-wing dictator. However, the Americans feared he would attack North Korea, so denied him the tanks and artillery he needed to invade the North. Meanwhile, Stalin was equipping the North Korean Army with plenty of these weapons. This led to an imbalance in forces between North and South Korea that encouraged Kim il Sung to invade the South to reunite Korea under communist rule.

There is much in this story over which historians have argued, but the issue that has divided them the most is whether Stalin encouraged Kim il Sung to invade South Korea in 1950. We know that Kim il Sung travelled to Moscow before the invasion to seek Stalin's support. What we do not know for certain is Stalin's response. The American historian John Lewis Gaddis is in no doubt that Stalin sanctioned the invasion: 'Stalin's "green light" to Kim il Sung was part of the larger strategy for seizing opportunities in East Asia that he had discussed with the Chinese: shortly after endorsing the invasion of South Korea, he encouraged Ho Chi Minh to intensify the Viet Minh offensive against the French in Indochina.' Other historians are not so sure. Burton Kaufman sees the war as a Korean civil war. Bruce Cummings argues that the Soviet Union had always been interested in Korea, and that what created a new strategic situation in the Far East was that, for the first time in its history, the United States was interested in it too.

Most historians agree that South Korea became the litmus test of America's resolve to contain communist expansion in Asia. As with Vietnam, the American commitment to South Korea sprang not from any rational analysis of its geo-strategic value, but from its symbolic value as a test of America's credibility.

Statement A

'The Korean War began because North Korea had a strong military advantage after being equipped by the USSR'.

Write your own amended version of this statement so as to reveal the complexity of the causes of the war.

Statement B

'War began in both Korea and Vietnam because of the USA's fear of communist expansion.'

Do you agree or disagree with this statement? If you agree, explain why. If you disagree, write your own amended version of this comparative statement.

On your own copy of the similarities/differences line shown on page 115, indicate where you think 'Why the Korean War started' should go.

---

2. Military aspects of the war

Nearly all the US military officers in Korea had fought in the Second World War. The same was not true of many of the ordinary soldiers because most of the American army had been demobilised since 1945. Therefore by 1950 the US Army was a shadow of its former self – ill-equipped and psychologically unprepared to fight a major war.

The terrain in Korea is very different from Vietnam. There is no jungle – in many places there is almost no vegetation. Much of Korea is mountainous (as is Vietnam), but Korea's mountains are barren, arid and dry. Korea's climate is extremely cold in winter and hot in summer. Unlike Vietnam, which has a monsoon season and is very humid, Korea has relatively little rainfall. If American soldiers in Vietnam complained that the fighting was difficult because of the torrential rain and the jungles, their predecessors had no such problems in Korea. In fact, Korea is just the sort of landscape where American technology and firepower could be brought to bear on their enemies. Or so you might think.

Korea has one other huge advantage over Vietnam as a place for America to fight a war. Unlike South Vietnam, South Korea is a peninsula surrounded by water on three sides. The only border to be defended was the border with North Korea, where the fighting was focused. So not only did America's UN forces have only one combat zone, but their navies could get around both sides of South Korea to support their land forces. Despite all these advantages, the Americans very nearly lost the Korean War, and it took all their skill and determination to stabilise the line around the 38th parallel.

The war on the ground

The most humiliating incident for the US Army in the Korean War was the headlong retreat of the 8th Army from the Chosin Reservoir. General MacArthur's forces had pursued the

△ American soldiers of the 35th Infantry Regiment watch as UN forces bombard enemy positions, February 1951.

△ US forces pioneered the use of helicopters in the Korean War.

North Koreans almost to the Chinese border but were heavily dependent on their supply lines, which were over-extended along narrow roads running through deep defiles between high mountains. The Chinese Army was primitive by comparison, but did not have the heavy equipment that tied the Americans to the roads. The Chinese swarmed over the hills and mountains, threatening to cut off the Americans from their line of retreat. Just five years after America's victory over Japan, 300,000 Chinese soldiers were chasing an American army down the Korean peninsula.

The main reason why the American/UN forces found this war so difficult was because of the huge number of Chinese committed to battle. They attacked in human waves, involving a prolific loss of life but often achieving their objectives. To clear a minefield, for instance, the leading elements of a Chinese attack were sacrificed. The Chinese approach is best illustrated by the example of the Battle of the Imjin River, where the British Gloucestershire Regiment, fighting in prepared positions on high ground with clear fields of fire, was simply overrun.

Two other major differences between Korea and Vietnam stand out:

1   Unlike in Vietnam, the United Nations supported the war in Korea. Over 15 countries sent troops to fight alongside the Americans.

2   Unlike in Vietnam, the UN did not face a major communist insurrection in South Korea.

The war in the air

As in Vietnam, the Americans had air superiority over the whole of Korea, but not total air supremacy. Korea saw the first sustained use of modern jet fighters in aerial combat as American F-86 Sabres engaged Korean MiG-15s. The MiGs took off from bases across the Yalu River in China – as in Vietnam, the communists could take sanctuary across a political border. For most of the time, however, the Americans and their UN allies dominated the skies over Korea.

The most controversial aspect of the aerial war was the effectiveness of strategic bombing. The US Air Force believed that strategic bombing could win the war. Like Rolling Thunder in Vietnam, Operation Strangle aimed at cutting off Chinese logistical support. Towards the end of the war, Operation Pressure Pump targeted North Korean power stations and dams, aimed at destroying the North Korean irrigation system, a tactic similar to Linebacker used 20 years later. The results were equally disappointing. North Korea had a primitive, pre-industrial economy with relatively few targets, getting most of

△ Korea saw the first sustained use of modern jet fighters like this US Navy F9F Panther.

One of the best films about the Korean War is *The Bridges at Toko-Ri*, starring James Holden and Grace Kelly. The film not only features excellent flying sequences, it also captures the unpopularity of the war and the strange discontinuity between the luxurious life pilots enjoyed in Japan and the risks taken on ground-attack missions.

its military supplies from Russia and China. Attempts to cut the railways and roads linking North Korea with China never halted the flow of supplies. The bombing may have helped force North Korea to negotiate the 1953 truce, but the US Air Force failed to learn from its experience in Korea that 'victory through air power' could not be achieved against a country like North Korea.

◁ **North Korea and China had the excellent Russian MiG-15.**

Statement A

'Korea was ideally suited to the American way of making war.'

Write your own amended version of this statement so as to reveal the complexity of the military problems facing America and its UN allies.

Statement B

'The military problems facing the USA in Korea were more straightforward than the ones it faced in Vietnam.'

Do you agree or disagree with this statement? If you agree, explain why. If you disagree, write your own amended version of this comparative statement.

On your own copy of the similarities/differences line shown on page 115, indicate where you think 'Military aspects of the war' should go.

---

3. Disagreements among American leaders about how the war should be fought

On 11 April 1951 Truman announced that he was relieving General MacArthur of his command. The clash between MacArthur and Truman represented more than just a clash of personalities. At its core lay a long-simmering resentment by military commanders of their oversight by civilian authority. MacArthur was a career soldier, born into a military family, used to giving orders. It was natural for him to trust his own judgement. This led him to question the judgement of his commander-in-chief in a way that was too public for Truman to ignore. The argument between Truman and MacArthur came down to two issues:

a) Should the USA extend the Korean War into China?

When the landing at Inchon forced the North Korean Army to retreat across the 38th parallel, it seemed obvious that the UN forces should pursue them into North Korea and eliminate the threat to South Korea's independence. The situation changed dramatically, however, when China intervened in the war. Truman was determined to limit the Korean War to Korea.

MacArthur disagreed. He believed that it was not enough to 'contain' communism, but that communism had to be defeated, not only in North Korea but in China, too. To that end he had requested – and been refused – permission to use nationalist Chinese forces from Formosa in the war in Korea. MacArthur believed North Korea's invasion proved that peaceful co-existence with communist China was impossible. Better, therefore, to fight while the USA still had the advantage in nuclear weapons.

b) Should the USA use the atomic bomb?

In November 1950, with the US Army in full retreat before the Chinese onslaught, MacArthur requested the use of 26 atomic bombs against military and industrial targets in North Korea and in communist China.

Profile: General Douglas MacArthur

General MacArthur was a legend in his own time. He served in the trenches during the First World War, where he was highly decorated for bravery. In the Second World War he was commander of the US Army in the Far East. For his defence of the Philippines he was awarded the Medal of Honour, America's highest decoration. He commanded the US Army as it fought its way through New Guinea to the Philippines. In September 1945 he officiated at Japan's surrender ceremony and was appointed Supreme Commander of the Allied Forces occupying Japan. When the Korean War broke out in 1950, he led the United Nations Command, masterminding the highly risky – and successful – American landing at Inchon.

Profile: President Harry Truman

In the First World War Truman served as an artillery officer in France. In 1935 he became a US senator for Missouri and in 1944 became vice president under President Roosevelt. When Roosevelt died on 12 April 1945, Truman became president. It was assumed that the war in the Far East would last until 1946. When the opportunity presented itself, Truman ended the war quickly by using atomic bombs against Japan. In the late 1940s he presided over enormous changes in US foreign policy, adopting a global outlook and committing the USA to the containment of communism. He presided over all the early crises of the Cold War. President Truman had a small sign on his desk saying 'The Buck Stops Here'.

Truman's attitude towards nuclear weapons had changed significantly since 1945; atomic bombs were only to be used as the last resort when the physical security of the United States was in immediate danger. Just a year earlier, in 1949, the Soviet Union had tested its first atomic bomb – another reason why America should show restraint. Yet many Americans agreed with MacArthur: if America possessed the means to win the war, why not use them? This argument surfaced again in Vietnam, but with less sincerity, reflecting greater public awareness of the consequences of nuclear warfare.

Statement A

'The major difference between Truman and MacArthur was about whether to spread the war into China.'

Write your own amended version of this statement so as to reveal the complexity of the disagreements among American leaders.

Statement B

'In both wars, Korea and Vietnam, there were fundamental disagreements between American soldiers and politicians about how the wars should be fought.'

Do you agree or disagree with this statement? If you agree, explain why. If you disagree, write your own amended version of this comparative statement.

On your own copy of the similarities/differences line shown on page 115, indicate where you think 'Disagreements among American leaders' should go.

4. The domestic reaction in the USA

As in Vietnam, the American army in Korea consisted of a disproportionately high number of men drawn from the lower middle class and working class. The USA had conscription, but the Selective Service Act allowed college students to avoid the draft. This bred resentment. With the United States enjoying economic prosperity, it was very difficult for ordinary soldiers and airmen in Korea to accept that the risks inherent in protecting the free world fell on their shoulders.

In January 1950 a public opinion poll reported that 49 per cent of the American public believed US participation in the Korean War was a mistake. According to a similar poll taken in August 1965, just 24 per cent of Americans thought the Vietnam War was a mistake. In other words, at the same stage in American involvement, six months into the fighting, the Korean War was more unpopular than the Vietnam War.

It is also worth considering that many people, including MacArthur, doubted the legality of America's intervention. There was no declaration of war in Korea, nor was Congress consulted. Truman took the United States to war as a member of the United Nations, in honour of its treaty commitments. This could have backfired badly with public opinion.

Why is it, then, that the Korean War did not provoke a significant antiwar movement? Where were the protest songs? Where were the street battles between antiwar protestors and the police? Where were the campus sit-ins, the burning draft cards, the marches and placards? Where was the hair?

Part of the explanation is simply that the Korean War was much shorter than Vietnam, three years as opposed to nine years. Yet the casualties were high – the USA lost 33,629 dead in Korea, as against 58,272 in Vietnam. Perhaps there was opposition to the war, but it did not have time to build up a head of steam and move onto the streets.

Another explanation is that Korea was less obviously a civil war than Vietnam. Despite the complex background and Syngman Rhee's unpopularity, North Korea's invasion and the atrocities committed by the communists appeared to confirm the general American view that communism aimed at destroying freedom by enslaving the world to a dangerous ideology.

Furthermore, the United States had UN support in Korea and was not isolated from world opinion. Years later, looking back on America's mistakes in Vietnam, Robert McNamara concluded that the USA should not have gone into Vietnam without the support of its allies. In Korea it had that support, with a UN resolution giving the war the legality of international law and the military support of thousands of UN troops.

Perhaps the main reason for the difference is that, unlike in Vietnam, the generation that fought in Korea had been 'militarised' in their minds by the Second World War and were far more deferential towards authority. The Korean War was fought before rock 'n' roll, before Students for a Democratic Society was founded, before television became widespread, before the civil rights movement made any significant headway. The generation that fought in Korea grew up in the hard world of the Great Depression and the Second World War.

The domestic context in the USA is another important factor. North Korea struck when the McCarthy era held the American people in its grip. In 1950 Julius and Ethel Rosenberg were arrested for passing nuclear secrets to the Russians. The House Committee on Un-American Activities was persecuting left-wing sympathisers, the very people who might have organised a protest movement. Voicing opposition to the Korean War might have been dangerous.

Nevertheless, there was some opposition to the Korean War. Most Americans had little understanding of what was happening in Korea, but they could see that America was not winning. The war's unpopularity expressed itself in demands that the United States should use every weapon in its arsenal to defeat the communists, encouraged by the rhetoric of Truman's Republican enemies.

5. How the war ended

By early 1952 it was clear that neither side was likely to win the Korean War. Both America and China had more or less accepted that there would be no major territorial changes.

Peace negotiations began in February 1952 at Panmunjom, which lay between the two armies. As in Vietnam, negotiations were complicated by the fact that the major powers were trying to negotiate over the heads of the regional powers involved in the dispute – North and South Korea – neither of which was willing to give up its claim to govern the entire country. In these circumstances a peace treaty to end the war was unattainable; all that could be hoped for was an armistice that would end the fighting, leaving the political argument unresolved.

The problem of prisoners of war

The main issue of the negotiations was the fate of prisoners of war (PoWs). The communists demanded that all Chinese and North Korean soldiers taken prisoner by the UN should be returned – on the face of it, a reasonable demand. But the Americans suspected that many of these prisoners would prefer to remain in the South and wanted to give them the option of choosing freedom over communism. Syngman Rhee was adamant that the Koreans among the prisoners should have the option of remaining in the South. These PoWs became a bargaining chip because of their symbolic value in the wider Cold War struggle between communism and the West.

The United Nations also insisted that every one of its prisoners be returned. In the event, 21 Americans, 1 Briton and 325 Koreans refused to be repatriated on the grounds that they had converted to communism. The story quickly got round that the communists had 'brainwashed' their prisoners through a combination of sleep deprivation, water torture and relentless ideological re-education.

Eventually a solution was found to this problem, which opened the path to an armistice. Prisoners who refused repatriation were entrusted to a neutral Repatriation Commission, where representatives of their own governments could visit them under supervision. If, after a further 30 days, they insisted on remaining behind, they were allowed to do so.

Why did the war intensify during peace negotiations?

As in Vietnam, both sides intensified the fighting during negotiations. The Americans bombed North Korea, especially the dams supplying the irrigation system for North Korean agriculture. The Chinese launched a major offensive to bring Syngman Rhee to his senses, for the South Korean president was refusing to cooperate with the Americans in ending the war.

As in Vietnam, the South Korean Government feared being sold out by the Americans. In some respects Rhee was as much of a nationalist megalomaniac as Kim il Sung: having got the support of a world superpower, Rhee tried to force the United States to fulfil his ambition to govern the whole of Korea. His argument was that South Korea would never be safe as long as the communists governed the North. When an agreement was reached at Panmunjom about a prisoner exchange, Rhee released all North Korean prisoners from his PoW camps, giving them the opportunity to vanish into the countryside. Most did. In the end the Americans had to threaten to abandon South Korea to its fate if its president did not accept terms.

The role of American politics

1952 was a presidential election year. Truman decided not to run and was succeeded as Democratic candidate by Adlai Stevenson. His Republican opponent was General Dwight D. Eisenhower, who had recently served as military commander of NATO. The election was fought in a febrile atmosphere. The McCarthy 'witch hunt' was drawing strength from the unpopular war in Korea. Eisenhower's election was a near-certainty after 20 years of Democratic rule, though his campaign was thrown into turmoil by accusations of financial corruption against Richard Nixon, his vice-presidential running mate. Nixon narrowly saved his political career with a national TV broadcast known as the 'Checkers Speech'.

The Korean War was an important issue in the 1952 election. Senator McCarthy attacked the Democrats for, as he saw it, failing to fight the war aggressively. Many Republicans criticised Truman for refusing to take the fight to the Chinese mainland or for refusing to use nuclear weapons. If elected, Eisenhower would help to silence the military resentment at civilian control. One month before the election Eisenhower announced that he would go to Korea to assess the situation, a promise he

> Watch Richard Nixon's Checkers Speech on YouTube: http://www.youtube.com/watch?v= EqjwBCH-vhY.
> It provides an insight into his character and ambition.

fulfilled in late November as president-elect. He concluded from this visit that a ceasefire was the most that could be hoped for.

Brinkmanship

Part of Eisenhower's strategy was to hand the war over to the South Koreans, a 'Koreanisation' of the conflict that might enable the USA to disengage. By the end of the war the South Korean Army stood at 665,000 but seemed incapable of fighting the communists by itself. Like Kissinger's 'madman theory' in Vietnam, the US secretary of state, John Foster Dulles, suggested to China that Eisenhower was prepared to use nuclear weapons to end the conflict. Eisenhower approved the use of nationalist Chinese forces from Formosa in commando raids against the Chinese mainland. MacArthur even suggested creating a radioactive zone between Korea and China that would kill anyone crossing the border, and although Eisenhower dismissed this suggestion out of hand, he would not rule out use of nuclear weapons. This was sound diplomacy that probably helped China and the Soviet Union apply pressure to North Korea to agree to terms.

Statement A

'The biggest obstacle to peace in Korea was Syngman Rhee.'

Write your own amended version of this statement so as to show the complexities of the peace negotiations in the Korean War.

Statement B

'It was more difficult to end the Korean War than to end the Vietnam War.'

Do you agree or disagree with this statement? If you agree, explain why. If you disagree, write your own amended version of this comparative statement.

On your own copy of the similarities/differences line shown on page 115, indicate where you think 'How the war ended' should go.

---

6. The historiography of the Korean War

So far we have compared the Korean and Vietnam Wars in terms of the wars themselves. It remains to compare the way historians have treated these two wars, especially how historians' interpretations have developed over time.

The first thing to recognise is that the Vietnam War had a major impact on Korean War historiography. Before Vietnam most historians agreed that the Korean War was the communists' fault, and that the American defence of South Korea was right and just. But once criticism of Vietnam was established as the orthodox interpretation of that war, it called into question the origins and meaning of the Korean conflict. Therefore the orthodox view of the Vietnam War created the revisionist interpretation of Korea. This knock-on effect of interpretation on interpretation can perhaps be understood most readily as the diagram below.

It will be apparent from this diagram that the historiography for Vietnam and Korea are mirror images of each other, entirely back to front. This reflects the fact that the dominating orthodox views of Korea and Vietnam were poles apart. Most major topics in history have a similar pattern: an orthodox point of view is established; in time historians challenge the orthodox view, offering a new perspective that historians call 'revisionist'; eventually a 'post-revisionist' view emerges that may return to the original orthodoxy while incorporating some amendments taken from revisionist arguments.

In the case of Vietnam, we questioned the extent to which these labels – orthodox and revisionist – could encompass the many historians who have written about the war, and we concluded that, by and large, the labels are indeed useful. The same is true for Korea. Students will find them useful in starting to make sense of the historical debates surrounding the Korean War.

Are the major issues in Vietnam historiography reflected in debates about the Korean War?

■ **Did political interference prevent the military from carrying out its mission in Korea?** MacArthur certainly thought so, and so did General Clarke, commander of UN forces at the time of the armistice. Korea was the first war that the United States did not 'win'. In Korea, much more than in Vietnam, the mission itself was in dispute: in Vietnam the military never suggested that the USA should deliberately attack communist China. In both wars the US Air Force was prevented from intensifying the bombing campaign as much as it would have liked by political considerations. However, the Korean War did not spawn a generation of disillusioned officers publishing criticisms of American policy.

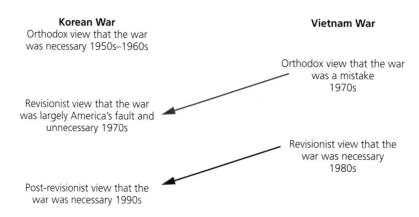

Korean War
Orthodox view that the war was necessary 1950s–1960s

Vietnam War
Orthodox view that the war was a mistake 1970s

Revisionist view that the war was largely America's fault and unnecessary 1970s

Revisionist view that the war was necessary 1980s

Post-revisionist view that the war was necessary 1990s

■ **Did arguments within the US administration undermine the American war effort in Korea?** Truman's decision to recall General MacArthur may have contributed to the defeat of the Democrats in the 1952 presidential election, as many Americans blamed Truman for failing to support the US military adequately.

■ **Has recent research into North and South Korea altered our view of the war?** Less so than in the case of Vietnam, partly because North Korea is still in the grip of Stalinist communism so access to North Korean records is well-nigh impossible. However,

recent research suggests that the rapid collapse of Syngman Rhee's forces in 1950 was partly due to his unpopularity.

■ **Has neoconservative revisionism overturned the orthodox view of the Korean War?** No, it hasn't. The orthodox view sees American intervention in the Korean War as a justified act of self-defence in a war that was encouraged – if not planned – by the Soviet Union and communist China. Two American historians have come to represent the differing viewpoints:

Bruce Cummings, the 'revisionist' author of The Origins of the Korean War (two volumes, 1981 and 1990), blamed the USA for attempting to establish a global hegemony after the Second World War, creating a 'great crescent' of capitalist nations stretching from Japan to India, out of which the concept of a 'defensive perimeter' emerged. In Cummings' view the perimeter was not defensive at all but aggressively capitalist and American. Cummings denied that Stalin instigated North Korea's attack on the South, arguing that Korea – like Vietnam – was a civil war. He argued that the US decision to attack north across the 38th parallel supports the view that American policy was aggressive, with some Americans spoiling for a fight with the Chinese.

John Lewis Gaddis, the 'orthodox' author of The Cold War (2005), rejected the idea that the USA was attempting to establish a global hegemony. He stressed the international dimension of the Korean War; documents recently released in the former Soviet Union show that Stalin did encourage Kim il Sung to attack South Korea. If anything, Vietnam War revisionism has come to the support of Korean War orthodoxy – both emphasise the very real threat posed by the Soviet Union and the essential rightness of America's response.

You may be wondering why it is not possible to lay these arguments to rest by looking at the evidence. Evidence in history rarely lays anything to rest, especially when modern politics is informing historians' opinions. History in America has become an intellectual battlefield upon which liberals and conservatives try to seize control of the past for present-day advantage. Much of the evidence is still locked away in North Korea. Anyway, the question whether or not Stalin 'ordered', 'approved', 'signalled his support for' or 'encouraged' Kim il Sung's invasion of South Korea is a question of semantics (the meaning of words), and may well be lost in translation.

■ Concluding your enquiry

Throughout this chapter you have been taking simple assertions and changing them to reveal the complexities about the Korean War. Now you need to use what you have learned to devise your own answer to the enquiry question: was the Korean War 'a rehearsal for Vietnam'? Your answer needs to incorporate your own, more complex, versions of the simple assertions in the chapter.

1 Look again at your similarities/differences line, which should now have six points marked on it.

2 Use these decisions to arrive at your own 'headline' answer to the question.

3 Now list twelve key points you would use from this enquiry to defend your generalisation, with supporting evidence.

4 Now write an essay to answer the question: was the Korean War 'a rehearsal for Vietnam'?

And finally … what do I think?

The Korean War certainly played a large part in creating the widespread view that communism was extremely dangerous. In the early 1960s Americans learned that the Chinese brainwashed American PoWs. It contributed to the mindset that made the Vietnam War itself not only likely but unavoidable – the idea that the USA would 'back off' and let the communists walk into South Vietnam was inconceivable. In this sense, Korea and Vietnam were part of the same long-term historical event, the Cold War. In both cases the USSR must have derived immense satisfaction from America's involvement in these wars. It was not until the Soviet Union itself got bogged down in Afghanistan in the 1980s that the United States was able to enjoy the spectacle of its arch-rival trapped in a quagmire of its own making.

To me, the Korean War holds many parallels with Vietnam. It is no accident that *M*A*S*H* (Mobile Army Surgical Hospital), the popular American sit-com set in the Korean War, is believed by many people to be a commentary on Vietnam. However, I would not take the parallels too far. In several important ways the Korean War was more serious than the Vietnam War. If Americans had died in Vietnam at the same rate at which they were killed in Korea, there would be 90,000 names on the Vietnam Veterans' Memorial Wall in Washington DC, not 56,000.

9 Conclusion
The time tunnel

The story of Hiroo Onoda

In 1974 a strange story swept the world's headlines. A Japanese soldier emerged from the Philippine jungle almost 30 years after the Second World War ended. Hiroo Onoda was an intelligence officer with the Imperial Japanese Army who did not know that the war was over. With three other soldiers, Onoda hid on the island of Lubang and carried on fighting. Over three decades he killed some 30 people. One by one his comrades surrendered, died or were killed, until he was the last one. He only surrendered when his former commanding officer travelled to Lubang and ordered him to give himself up.

Onoda returned to a hero's welcome in Japan, where his loyalty to the emperor was praised. In 1974 Hirohito was still Emperor of Japan, but he was no longer regarded as a god. Many other things had changed. Onoda knew nothing of the atomic bombs dropped on Japanese cities. He knew nothing of jet aircraft, television, penicillin, the Cold War or the space race. But what he found most difficult to accept were the changes that had taken place in Japan itself. When he joined the Army in 1942, Japan was a deeply traditional, religious country, full of wood-and-paper houses, old-fashioned industries and medieval agriculture, governed by the Army. The country he returned to was a nation of skyscrapers and bullet trains, neon signs, baseball, fast food and electronics, with a democratically elected government. His beloved Japan had been

△ Hiroo Onoda surrendering to Philippine officials in 1974.

Americanised. Hiroo Onoda was unable at first to accept these changes. In 1975 he moved to Brazil and became a farmer. Ten years later he came back to Japan and ran camps for Japanese children, teaching them how to survive in the great outdoors – he was an expert on that subject. He died in 2014, aged 91.

Hiroo Onoda's story is one of the strangest personal tales of the twentieth century. His return to Japan must be as close to time travel as anyone is ever likely to get, literally stepping out of the 1940s into the world of the future. Of course, lots of people lived through those 30 years and experienced those changes, but saw them unfolding, one step at a time. Onoda's tale serves to remind us that time moves on, that change is inevitable, and that people must adapt to change or end up – as many old people do – living in their memories of the past.

■ **Enquiry Focus:** Did the United States achieve the objectives for which it fought the Vietnam War?

Today we look back on the Vietnam War from the perspective of a half a century of changes – some for the better, some for the worse. In many ways the world that shaped the Korean and Vietnam Wars no longer exists. The Cold War with the Soviet Union ended in the late 1980s. The Soviet Union itself collapsed in 1991. In the Far East, 'globalisation' has led to the rapid development of the 'Pacific Rim' nations – Vietnam, South Korea and China especially. This massive shift in the world economy forces us to consider the possibility that the United States got what it wanted after all.

1 The final enquiry in this book is rather different from the others. In this chapter you will be given signposts for independent learning. We will start you off by giving you a headstart in your investigation, but it will be up to you to research each issue, using any resources available to you – textbooks, the internet, library books, documentaries. For each issue you will be given a short summary of the issue and one or two 'signposts' – guidance about what to look for and where to look.

2 When you have done your research, place each issue on a sliding bar chart like the one below. The higher you choose to place each issue on the chart, the closer the USA has got to achieving its aims.

3 Once you have completed the bar chart, write an answer to the enquiry question.

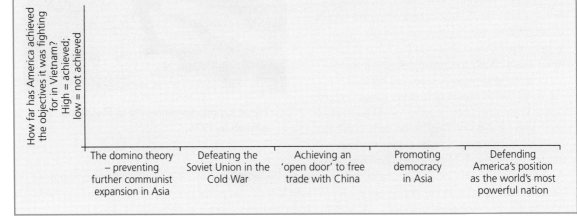

The time tunnel

Imagine you are a time traveller hurtling through a rift in the temporal vortex. The diagram above shows you the main events that have occurred in the Far East since the end of the Vietnam War.

In your time machine you can visit these events in order to discover more about them. The time machine is, of course, your research.

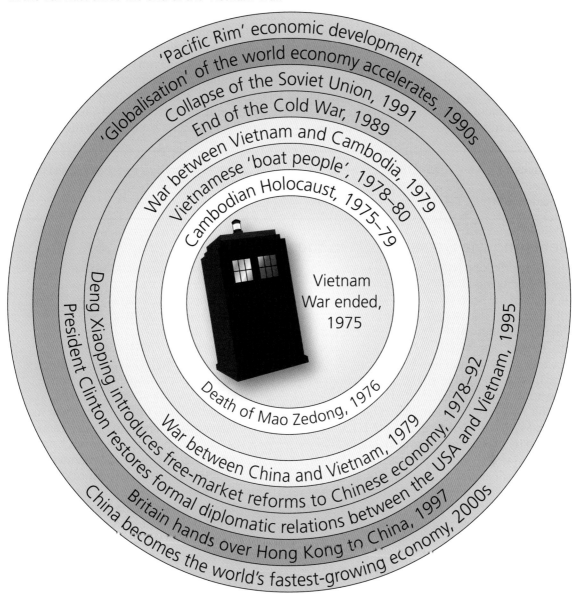

'Pacific Rim' economic development

'Globalisation' of the world economy accelerates, 1990s

Collapse of the Soviet Union, 1991

End of the Cold War, 1989

War between Vietnam and Cambodia, 1979

Vietnamese 'boat people', 1978–80

Cambodian Holocaust, 1975–79

Vietnam War ended, 1975

Death of Mao Zedong, 1976

Deng Xiaoping introduces free-market reforms to Chinese economy, 1978–92

President Clinton restores formal diplomatic relations between the USA and Vietnam, 1995

War between China and Vietnam, 1979

Britain hands over Hong Kong to China, 1997

China becomes the world's fastest-growing economy, 2000s

The domino theory – preventing further communist expansion in Asia

In 1975, as the Vietnam War came to an end, a disaster was unfolding across the border in Cambodia. Destabilised by the war, Cambodia fell into the hands of the Khmer Rouge, a radical communist group led by the totalitarian dictator

Pol Pot. The Khmer Rouge tried to completely erase the history of Cambodia in order to impose a form of primitive agrarian communism – starting with a new 'Year Zero', the urban population of Phnom Penh and other towns was forcibly relocated to the fields to work on collective farms. Anyone associated with the old history of Cambodia was murdered, including – for example – anyone who spoke French, the former colonial language.

Alarmed by these developments, in 1979 Vietnam invaded Cambodia to overthrow Pol Pot's regime. Vietnam's invasion alarmed the United States, which feared the domino theory might be coming true. It also alarmed China; in 1979 China attacked Vietnam and fought a brief border war as a warning not to attempt to reunite the whole of French Indochina under Vietnamese rule. This was interesting because it confirmed that Vietnam and China were old enemies, and suggested that if America had left Vietnam alone, China would have 'contained' Vietnam.

The Cambodian–Vietnamese War lasted from 1979 to 1991, when the Paris Peace Accords handed over power briefly to a UN mission. The UN withdrew after elections, but in 1997 a military coup established the Cambodian People's Party under Prime Minister Hun Sen. Today Cambodia has been described by the historian David Roberts as a 'vaguely communist free-market state with a relatively authoritarian coalition ruling over a superficial democracy'.

Signpost: *The Killing Fields* (1984), directed by Roland Joffe, is a graphic reconstruction of Pol Pot's murderous regime, based on the true story of the American photographer Sydney Schanberg and his Cambodian friend Dith Pran.

Defeating the Soviet Union in the Cold War

The most profound political change since 1975 has been the end of the Cold War and the downfall of the Soviet Union. As we have seen (Chapter 5), in the 1970s détente with the Soviet Union made it possible for the USA to get out of Vietnam. Détente suffered a major setback, however, in 1979 when the USSR invaded Afghanistan. This led to a new Cold War and a new arms race in the early 1980s.

The American president, Ronald Reagan, hoped to push the Soviet Union into economic collapse by developing a new generation of high-tech weapons. These weapons included cruise missiles, antiballistic missiles, stealth aircraft, laser-guided munitions and even particle beam weapons (which never really worked). The USSR was facing bankruptcy for many reasons, one of which was its efforts to keep up with the Americans. Russia was also fighting its own 'Vietnam War', in Afghanistan, and faced major economic and systemic problems that existed long before Reagan came to office. In 1985 a new Soviet premier, Mikhail Gorbachev, decided to improve relations with the USA and reform the Soviet Union through policies called glasnost and perestroika (openness and restructuring).

As Gorbachev reformed the Soviet Union, Soviet–American relations improved. In 1989 Gorbachev let it be known that Russia would no longer intervene to prop up unpopular communist governments in eastern Europe. This led to democratic revolutions across eastern Europe, the fall of the Berlin Wall and the collapse of the Iron Curtain. Then in 1991, following an attempted military coup by disaffected communists, the Soviet Union itself broke up into the Russian Federation and a number of independent states, including Ukraine, the Baltic States, Belarus and others.

It could be argued that the Vietnam War played an important part in thwarting the Soviet Union's designs, and that it contributed to America's 'victory' in the Cold War. Eventually the USA got what it wanted, an end to the Soviet domination of eastern Europe. However, as I write this sentence, a civil war is being fought in the eastern Ukraine as Russia tries to regain some of its lost territory and status.

Signpost: The BBC's History website has a Cold War section where you can find articles on the fall of the Soviet Union: www.historylearningsite.co.uk/coldwar.htm.

Achieving an 'open door' to free trade with China

Following the death of Mao Zedong in 1976 and a brief period when the so-called 'Gang of Four' governed China, Deng Xiaoping began reforming China's economy. His aim was to introduce more of a free market, giving the Chinese people greater freedom to manufacture, buy and sell according to capitalist principles. As he predicted, his reforms have transformed China into the 'workshop of the world'. China now produces the vast majority of the consumer products purchased in the West.

In the early twentieth century the USA hoped to achieve an 'open door' to China, and to a large extent this has now been achieved. But the boot is on the other foot – Americans longed for the day when China would open its doors to American manufactured goods, giving US industry a vast new market for its products. The opposite has happened: American (and British) companies have relocated their suppliers to China, where manufacturing costs are much lower than in the West. This has led to cheaper products for American consumers, but higher unemployment in the United States.

China is not the only beneficiary of this globalisation of the world economy. South Korea is one of four so-called 'tiger economies' in the Far East. Vietnam also supplies many of the world's goods. A visitor to Vietnam today might conclude that the Americans had won the war after all.

> **Signpost:** This is a website for potential investors in the Pacific Rim economies, and especially in the four 'tiger economies' – Hong Kong, South Korea, Singapore and Taiwan: www.investopedia.com/terms/p/pacific-rim.asp. You can find out more about the Pacific Rim and economic tigers by going to www.geograph.about.com.

Promoting democracy in Asia

As I write, pro-democracy demonstrators in Hong Kong are protesting about China's decision to limit their freedom of choice in elections. When Britain handed over Hong Kong to China in 1997, it was on the understanding that Hong Kong's free institutions would continue to function as a special zone under Chinese sovereignty. Now it appears that China is seeking to limit candidates to those acceptable to the Chinese Government.

In 1989 a much more serious event took place in Tiananmen Square in Beijing, the Chinese capital. Pro-democracy demonstrators, encouraged by Gorbachev's reforms in the Soviet Union, occupied the square. The Chinese authorities dithered at first, then decided to crack down on the demonstrators and sent in the Army. The demonstration turned into a massacre. China's communist leaders appear determined to hold onto power despite their economic reforms.

Elsewhere in Asia democracy has had some success, particularly in South Korea and, of course, Japan.

> **Signpost:** Kate Adie was the BBC correspondent in Tiananmen Square and reported live as the massacre unfolded. Watch her report on YouTube: search for Katie Adie Tianamen Square. You can also read her account of the massacre in her autobiography, *The Kindness of Strangers* (2003).

Defending America's position as the world's most powerful nation

The collapse of the Soviet Union left the United States as the 'last superpower standing', a position uniquely powerful. The USA still enjoys the world's largest economy, and its military power is unrivalled around the world. But how much longer can it maintain this advantage?

Most of the heavy primary and secondary industries that sustained American power in the twentieth century have vanished. The USA tries to sustain an enormous defence budget, but in doing so has run up trillions of dollars of debt. For example, in the 1980s President Reagan reactivated the old Second World War American battleship *Missouri*, the ship on which the Japanese surrendered in 1945 – but to do it, he had to borrow money from Japan! Today communist China underwrites America's financial system despite the fact that the USA still defends Formosa against Chinese invasion, and South Korea against communist attack. Many observers predict that in the not-too-distant future, the United States will find itself struggling to hold on to its superpower status.

> **Signpost:** Paul Kennedy, *The Rise and Fall of the Great Powers* (1987). The final chapter of Kennedy's book predicted that, in the first half of this century, China would replace the United States as the world's largest economy. Are his predictions coming true?

> **Signpost:** Niall Ferguson, *Colossus: The Rise and Fall of the American Empire* (2004). According to Ferguson, the USA is an empire 'running on empty'.

And finally …

North Korea is the last Stalinist nation in the world. In 2001 President George W. Bush referred to North Korea as part of the 'axis of evil' facing the modern world. While all these astounding changes have taken place in the Far East, the one element that seems not to have changed at all is North Korea. In the *Telegraph Magazine*, on 10 October 2014, there was an article about a young woman named Yeonmi Park who fled from North Korea and now lives in the South. Part of the article read as follows:

> Yeonmi Park was nine years old when she was invited to watch her best friend's mother be shot … Yeonmi watched in horror as the woman she knew was lined up alongside eight other prisoners and her sentence was read out. Her crime was having watched South Korean films and lending the DVDs to friends.

Look at a photograph of Korea taken at night from space. China, South Korea and Japan are lit up like Christmas trees. North Korea is discernible only by its complete absence of light – its economy is totally stagnant. Its rulers govern through fear, as they have done since 1948. And ever since 1953 an American army has stood watch in South Korea, defending that country against the possibility of another North Korean attack.

This is my old friend Jake Helms. I took the black-and-white photograph in 1970. In 1974 Jake joined the US Army and was sent to Korea as part of the ongoing American commitment to the defence of the South. His equipment in this photograph is vintage Vietnam-era: M-1 helmet, combat fatigues, boots and an M-16 rifle. This photograph reminds me that Korea and Vietnam were not just 'events in history', but that they involved real people whose lives were deeply affected. It also reminds me that these two wars were linked by the long-term American commitment to the defence of Asia against the communist threat. Jake knows many people who fought in Vietnam, one of whom told him a story about his experience as a gunner on a Huey helicopter gunship. Jake tells the story better than I could; I will leave the final words to him, as told to me in a recent letter:

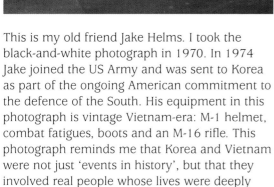

First story involves patrol of the Ho Chi Minh Trail. As you know this was the supply line from the North to the South. At the time Frank was a door gunner on a Huey. An M-60 machine gun was mounted on each side door. The gun fires 7.62 mm rounds. I have fired one before. It's a cool gun. The M-60's nickname is 'pig' because of the amount of ammo it uses.

There were no rules of engagement at this time so if it moved, kill it. After all that is the Army's job. Kill people and break things. The Viet Cong were using elephants to transport material from the North to the South. Vital to the VC to get these supplies.

Frank and his team would take out any supply column they saw. Told me he would aim for the elephants. When the 7.62 rounds hit the elephants he said it looked like dust popping off the animals. Of course the dust was blood. All I could think of at the time was 'poor elephants'. Frank reminded me that if the supplies reached their destination more of our guys would die.

To be honest I am very tired. Not that I don't care but I am getting too old to worry. I have seen many things, good and bad. Have travelled to different places. I have experienced life. So if the shit hits the fan, so be it.

Index